T0150473

Dark Academia

'Within the last 50 years, neoliberalism has waged a major assault on higher education. The seriousness of this assault and its impact on modes of governance, faculty, and students is a narrative of major importance that needs to be identified, analysed, and addressed in all of its complexities if higher education is to be reclaimed as a crucial public good. At last, we have a book that does just that. With *Dark Academia*, Peter Fleming has written a brilliant exposé of the scourge of neoliberalism and its dark transformation of higher education into an adjunct of sordid market forces. This is a book that should be read by anyone concerned with not only higher education but the fate of critically engaged agents, collective resistance, and democracy itself.'

—Henry Giroux, McMaster University Chair for Scholarship
in the Public Interest & The Paulo Freire Distinguished
Scholar in Critical Pedagogy

'Our foremost critic of management ideology, Peter Fleming, turns his talents to the corporate university and what he rightly calls its authoritarian turn, and he does so with devastating results.'

—Stefano Harney, Honorary Professor, Institute of Gender,
Sexuality, Race and Social Justice, University of British Columbia

Also available by Peter Fleming:

The Death of Homo Economicus:
Work, Debt and the Myth of Endless Accumulation

'Sparklingly sardonic ... Hilariously angry.'
Guardian

'An outstanding analysis of economics, society and
the human condition.'
Morning Star

The Mythology of Work:
How Capitalism Persists Despite Itself

'Thought-provoking.'
The Times

'The practical lesson from Fleming's provocation is to ask
ourselves how much of the work we do every day is simply
posturing and bad habit.'
Financial Times

'Acerbic, darkly humorous ... an entertaining read.'
Times Higher Education

Dark Academia

How Universities Die

Peter Fleming

PLUTO PRESS

First published 2021 by Pluto Press
New Wing, Somerset House, Strand, London WC2R 1LA

www.plutobooks.com

British Library Cataloguing in Publication Data
A catalogue record for this book is available from the British Library

ISBN   978 0 7453 4105 7   Hardback
ISBN   978 0 7453 4106 4   Paperback
ISBN   978 1 7868 0813 4   PDF eBook
ISBN   978 1 7868 0814 1   EPUB eBook

This book is printed on paper suitable for recycling and made from fully
managed and sustained forest sources. Logging, pulping and manufacturing
processes are expected to conform to the environmental standards of the
country of origin.

Typeset by Stanford DTP Services, Northampton, England

Simultaneously printed in the United Kingdom and United States of America

Contents

Introduction: Infinite Hope ... But Not for Us   1

1. Dark Academia   6
2. La La Land   20
3. Welcome to the Edu-Factory   34
4. The Authoritarian Turn in Universities   50
5. You're Not a Spreadsheet With Hair   66
6. The Demise of *Homo Academicus*   83
7. High Impact ...   97
8. The Academic Star-Complex   112
9. Student Hellscapes   126
10. How Universities Die   141

Conclusion: Are Some Lost Causes Truly Lost?   158

Notes   166
Index   202

Introduction
Infinite Hope ... But Not for Us

I was completing the first draft of this book when the Covid-19 virus was reclassified a global pandemic and all hell broke loose. Universities around the world were soon closed and staff raced to transfer classes online, sometimes within a few days. Erstwhile technophobes became experts in virtual technology overnight. Only after the situation stabilised and teaching resumed on Zoom were the stark fiscal implications considered. With so many international students unable to travel and campuses shut, higher education would soon face a bleak financial future as gaping budget deficits loomed.

Ominous predictions have been posited about what the post-Covid-19 scenario will look like in the years to come. According to leading business commentator Scott Galloway, none but a small group of elite institutions will survive in their present form. The rest will be transformed into 'Zombie Universities' as funding shrinks and mid/lower-range colleges limp on before finally succumbing to the inevitable.[1] Senior managers in most universities have already sounded the alarm, announcing significant pay-cuts, redundancies and major downsizing plans. And no doubt the crisis will be used as a convenient alibi for regressive interventions that some technocrats had always wanted to implement but daren't until now. It looks like we're about to witness an academic bloodletting on an unprecedented scale.

This is not exactly what I had in mind when writing the book, an examination of how universities die. Upon rereading the chapters through this lens, mostly written before anyone had ever heard of Coronavirus, the arguments take on a rather sinister tone, which is unintended. However, the more astute commentaries about Covid-19 make an important point: modern universities were *already* gravely ill.[2] The founding mission of public higher education has been pulverised over the last 35 years as universities morphed into business enterprises obsessed with income, growth and outputs. Hence the high-risk strategy regarding the lucrative international student market, a bubble that's been threatening to burst for some time.

Internal work cultures have been dramatically altered too. Just look at the book titles that academics write about their own profession: *The Toxic University* … *The Great Mistake* … *A Perfect Mess* … *University in Ruins* … *The Lost Soul of Higher Education* … *Lower Ed* … and my personal favourite, *Whackademia*.[3]

Is the doom and gloom warranted? Yes, probably.

Impersonal and unforgiving management hierarchies have supplanted academic judgement, collegiality and professional common sense. In many institutions, senior executives have no

PhDs and have been trained in business or the military instead. Mindless performance targets dominate teaching and research to the point of caricature, designed by functionaries who've never taught a class or written a research article in their lives. Unfortunately, these hierarchies have become notoriously bossy. Coercion rather than volition compels much academic labour today, even tasks that scholars would have otherwise done willingly because it's central to their vocation. This surfeit of duress, most of which is unnecessary and counterproductive, is a defining feature of the corporate university. Making matters worse, more than 70 per cent of teaching staff are employed on zero-hour contracts that were perfected in the gig-economy.[4] But even tenured academics are wilting under the pressure, too afraid to speak out and wracked with anxiety about their publication pipeline.

To reiterate, clearly the modern university was already at death's door before the pandemic struck, before Zoom, Kaltura and Panopto became academic household brands. Covid-19 simply threw these dire conditions into sharp relief for all to see. And this brings me to the purpose of the book. The hidden psychosomatic injuries that accompany this lingering demise – as endured by countless students and academics deep inside the contemporary university – have yet to be properly catalogued and explained. So that's what I will endeavour to do.

A brief essay I published in 2019 called 'Dark Academia' formed the germ of the main idea. It tried to confront the dark side of working and studying in the modern university, calling out trends that are hardly ever mentioned officially. The essay drew on my own personal experiences, being careful to anonymise the examples and incidences. When published it attracted some attention from fellow travellers, many of whom agreed with the basic premise. Besides messages of support, however, four other kinds of correspondence stood out for me, which reinforce the arguments I wish to make here.

The first was from academics informing me that the grim picture I painted of the neoliberal university was nothing compared to their own experiences. While I assumed that tales of burnout, Uber-like ratings of lecturers and vindictive managers offered an accurate (albeit pessimistic) impression of higher education today, these academics said I hadn't gone far enough. After describing encounters in their own universities, sometimes in graphic and distressing detail (e.g., 'dirty protests' in faculty bathrooms, senior management announcing plans to burn its library books to free up more teaching space, etc.), I thought … my god! What kind of institutional pressures have permitted such horrors to occur and in some instances be normalised as run-of-the-mill?

The second type of response was equally depressing. These fellow academics didn't bother with the substance of the argument. They were more interested in identifying exactly who the anonymised individuals and universities dotted throughout my essay were. In other words, they wanted to gossip. Whether innocuous or malign, I believe this rather disappointing pastime is so prevalent in academia today because political dialogue has largely been pushed underground. Organisational gossip is symptomatic of this lack of formal voice. And we know where it can lead if mixed with competitive rivalry and resentment.

The third response was related. It reflects how universities have recently embraced authoritarian management structures, sometimes bizarrely so. Fear is now the go-to technique for motivating faculty and staff. Managers choose this method since it's far easier to issue orders fait accompli via email than talk with colleagues and build a consensus. These edicts, even when courteously worded, carry an implicit threat regarding non-compliance. At any rate, this reaction to my essay simply asked whether I was worried about being fired. The sentiment demonstrates how far universities have moved from a collegium of peers to hierarchical business enterprises. Vocal opposition – even in an esoteric journal far removed from the public eye – is risky.

Under such circumstances people inevitably self-censor to avoid the nasty side of technocracy. This touches on a central theme in the book. What I call the 'boss syndrome' not only distinguishes senior administrators, where academics are viewed as hired labour who can be replaced at a moment's notice. No, sadly this mindset has infiltrated the workforce too, shaping how they see themselves and their jobs.

The fourth response even I – an inveterate pessimist – found disturbing. Once again, the essential thesis of the essay was ignored. Instead I received emails from academics demanding to know why I hadn't referenced them. They had made related conjectures too one ambitious junior professor insisted, so surely I should have cited their insightful work. Hell, I thought, have things gotten *that* bad? Colleagues who ought to have known better had totally swallowed the lure of competitive careerism, spurred on by crass incentive systems that even McKinsey and Co would find distasteful. It is lamentable that even scholars who are ardent critics of the neoliberal university still rejoice when their Google Scholar Citation Score increases and would seemingly run over their next of kin in a small jeep if it meant getting published in a 'top' journal.

What are the alternatives? The problem is not a lack of better models for governing universities, particularly public ones. There are plenty of those available, some of which we will discuss. No. The trouble is how we might realise them given how embedded the present system now is. Corporatisation has been so exhaustive (on a financial, organisational, individual and subjective level) that reversing it in the current context feels nearly impossible. Rather than fighting back, most academics have merely found ways to dwell in the ruins. This intense undercurrent of resignation, whether warranted or not, sets the scene for what I term dark academia.

1

Dark Academia

1.

Snow was falling hard in London and the streets were treacherous. Upon leaving my apartment that morning I wondered whether the inner city demo might be called off. Luckily it wasn't. I met up with some colleagues at a pub and then joined the thousands of university workers on strike. The 2018 UK pensions' dispute had been smouldering for a while. Employers were stubbornly sticking to their plans to eviscerate our pension scheme. As the march began – winding its way through the frozen city towards Parliament Square – war stories were shared among friends and strangers. Some HR departments had upped the ante, claiming teachers could be personally liable for missed classes if students demanded a refund. Coventry University established a private subsidiary – Coventry University Group – with its own company union or Staff Consultative Group. They effectively barred the national union from representing its lecturers.[1] Ugly terms and conditions followed. Reports of other underhanded tactics were shared among the crowd as we huddled together and rubbed our hands for warmth.

A number of things occurred to me that day. The strike had revealed some unpleasant truths. Call me naive, but up until then I hadn't really seen the university as a stereotypical 'employer' who stood over its workers shaking a stick. Packing shelves in supermarkets as a teenager, yes. But universities were supposed to be striving towards a very different governance ideal, a community of equals where those at the top of the ladder were simply an elevated version of 'us'. Not anymore it would seem. All of a sudden the fluffy rhetoric about collegiality evaporated as dark suited bosses and their HR footsoldiers began snarling at us. I'd been wrong to assume that an academic vocation was different to working for Accenture. The kind of occupational solidarity I believed fundamental to the job was completely out of sync with the times.

This misfit between expectations (academic values) and the brave new world of higher education is one reason why universities have become such sad places to work. A recent survey of 6000 UK academics revealed a whopping 90 per cent were 'very unsatisfied' with university management.[2] Stress, lack of respect, minimal voice and low trust were common reasons why. The problem is that academics are highly trained specialists who've dedicated years of painstaking study on their chosen discipline. Nobody in the organisation is more knowledgeable about their teaching and research area, including line-managers. Simple top-down hierarchies don't work in this setting and generally piss people off. And unlike manual workers who must produce X number of widgets, academic labour is abstract and can't be prompted by factory-like performance incentives. Yet they pervade the sector with a vengeance.

The *pre*-neoliberalised university aspired to collegial self-governance not because it was 'nicer' – often the opposite – but because it was the best way to organise a workforce with these idiosyncratic attributes. The ideology of managerialism radically revoked this idea. Instead of originating from the academic community as elected peers (to which they would eventually return), a detached cadre of managers now circulate within the higher education industry, moving from institution to institution, having little in common with the scholars they oversee.

2.

The militancy displayed by workers during the pensions dispute came out of nowhere and was a major surprise. Like others, I'd partially written off rebellion in the corporate university. Years of economic rationalisation had irrevocably splintered and fragmented the profession. Hence the dark mood of defeatism in academe. Employers had succeeded in transforming higher education into a de facto capitalist industry – an 'Edu-Factory' – and resistance was futile.[3] But not so fast. After the strikes a modicum of optimism crept back into the workforce, cruel perhaps but unmistakeable. University management eventually backed down and agreed to reconsider their plans for our pensions. Everyone returned to work and it looked like victory for our union. I left England not long after.

About a year later some friends told me that trouble was brewing again. Workers were returning to the picket lines, with pensions again the central grievance. It seemed that the initial management concession was a ploy to defuse the momentum generated by the first strike. They bargained it would be difficult to repeat this after everything had returned to normal. That's when employers pushed for pension cuts again, only this time with increased belligerence. At Liverpool University, staff were informed they'd have to make up missed classes or face serious penalties. Pay had already been deducted during the strike, so this meant working for nothing. Similar strong-arm tactics were levelled at students too. Those who either joined the strikes or refused to cross picket lines, a letter from the Liverpool University Vice Chancellor warned, 'will be marked as absent, which will have an effect on [their] attendance record'.[4] International students would jeopardise their visas as a consequence.

The British pensions dispute is not a unique case. Industrial action has occurred in other countries as higher education providers seek to squeeze cost-savings from the workforce and ramp up productivity. For instance, US adjuncts languish on terrible pay and conditions. They've launched protests at several colleges over the past few years, including Cincinnati, Montclair State, Point Park among others. These promising moments of revolt led some to predict that an 'adjunct revolt' might soon be underway.[5]

But it was a false dawn. No sector-wide movement has emerged to challenge the hyper-exploitation that's been routinised in US colleges and universities. Even when the profession enjoyed its most powerful opportunity – during the Covid-19 crisis as universities became totally reliant on academic goodwill and unpaid overtime – most unions simply kowtowed and got to work.

This is an important point. Notwithstanding the UK pensions strike, the unhappiness sweeping higher education in the US, UK, Australasia, Canada and many European countries has rarely resulted in effective counter-planning and resistance. Some even talk about *academic zombies* on this score, which is a bit harsh.[6] Nevertheless, the higher education workforce has proven remarkably lousy at translating their frustration into a sustained movement, a conundrum this book will try to explain. Without a unified voice, the despair has been pushed underground instead, a problem for individuals to deal with alone as they bear heavier teaching loads, more emails, deteriorating pay and conditions and the unstoppable march of managerialism.

Sure, we can identify a few isolated and occasional victories. And once again, it's not as if academics aren't getting stroppy. Think here of the scolding open letter sent to the UK government by 126 prominent professors in 2015.[7] It didn't change anything. There's a general sense that the overall war has been lost and higher education is teetering on the brink of something much worse. The 2020 Covid-19 pandemic didn't alter that view, on the contrary.

While we have a decent understanding of what's objectively gone wrong in higher education, less attention has been paid to the psychological and emotional toll that 35 years of funding cuts and creeping technocracy has had on staff and students. In exploring this dimension, the book presents a doleful assessment. Moreover, exactly how we might crawl from the wreckage, one that seems fairly complete, is not entirely clear. Hence why the recent wave of optimism that's appeared on this question is somewhat premature. Several writers contend that we can still salvage the university and its progressive agenda.[8] Eminently sensible roadmaps for radical change are then posited. But let's face it. Try being a 'slow professor' today and you'll soon be on the wrong end of a pink slip. That's my point: the principles of neoliberalism are now so entrenched that one has to wonder whether the modern university is capable (nay, *worth*) being saved.

I know the familiar retort. One cannot be critical without proposing alternatives, et cetera. But that's something I'll only reluctantly do given the rubble before us. This book is therefore an exercise in *uni-pessimism*, justified by very real and concrete trends. It is time to ask the old Kantian question of whether hope itself is admissible when it comes to one of our most revered establishments.[9] For all intents and purposes, the bad guys have won. And if so, perhaps it's time to consider beginning again and escape the impenetrable darkness that's eclipsing the academy today.

3.

Contemporary critics of the neoliberal university face three challenges.

First, the most successful arguments against higher education today – that are actually being listened to and acted upon by power-holders – are not coming from the left. Instead neo-conservatives and libertarian right-wingers are making the biggest ripples in this respect.[10] University bashing has become a favourite pastime in these camps. That was evident during the Covid-19 pandemic. Cato Institute analyst, Bryan Caplan, implied the crisis could help expose the systemic failures of higher education in America.[11] The same attitude might also explain why governments around the world excluded universities from 'job keeper' financial aid as the pandemic spread and staff were fired. Best to let the market work its magic instead and streamline an industry that's weighed down by thousands of needless 'bullshit jobs'.

In light of this enmity, any progressive and emancipatory re-evaluation of higher education must carefully sidestep the reactionary right-wing pessimism that's helped lay waste to tertiary education over the past several decades. One of the staunchest critics of the neoliberal university today remain neoliberals themselves! Even as the sector buckles under the weight of extreme commercialisation, pundits continue to believe that universities need further market reforms to fix this now highly dysfunctional industry. That marketisation is a root cause of these dysfunctions is unimportant to them.[12]

It's easy to spot libertarians like Ben Shapiro and Bryan Caplan when they start laying into the university with puerile accusations. The situation gets murkier, however, when pro-market theorists deploy left-sounding lamentations about the 'corporate university', only to conclude (in the name of pragmatism and 'you gotta know the territory') that institutions must adapt and work within these constraints.[13]

In any case, the political terrain we must traverse isn't simply divided between those 'for' or 'against' the corporate university. Matters are more complex.

Second, one cannot ignore the fact that academics themselves have often played the neoliberal game, seduced by competitive careerism and its incentive systems, hoping to come out on top or even famous. Don't get me wrong, the 'publish or perish' directive is *very real* and limits our options to act otherwise. Faculty are terminated or denied tenure on these grounds. By the same token, however, this is not entirely a story of helpless victims. I'm not just talking about the few career psychopaths prowling the academy, who'd gladly walk over a grandparent if it meant landing a major journal publication. No, I'm referring to the silent majority, reasonable and otherwise self-aware scholars who have, often out of necessity, quietly internalised the new dogma, leaning on it as the default option for how the profession works.

Reversing corporatisation is thus difficult when individual careers are pegged to its key mechanisms, perpetuated even by those who end up angry and frustrated by those mechanisms. For example, I'm still surprised that when I suggest journal rankings ought to be abandoned given how divisive they are, some colleagues remain hesitant: 'that's going a bit too far isn't it – we still need some sort of quality measure don't we?' Careers and occupations have been thoroughly tied to the fetish of 'top-tier' journals, even among those who feel disadvantaged by the arrangement, which indicates how tough it will be to undo the precepts of academic capitalism.[14] But one thing is patently obvious. That single-authored journal articles (trapped behind giant paywalls) are now considered the pinnacle of scholarly excellence indicates just how vanquished this workforce really is.

Third, universities (especially the public ones) are obviously beholden to their governmental overseers, funding ministries and associated agencies. To a significant extent, we cannot oppose the contemporary university without problematising the state apparatus itself, including its recent dalliance with alt-right politics and authoritarianism. And that's a tall order. Undoubtedly some universities were enamoured with the idea of imitating business conglomerates and needed little persuasion. For most, however, the real drivers were radical governmental policies. In North America, the UK, Australasia and elsewhere education ministers/secretaries have been brash advocates of commercialisation for several decades. Decrease funding and ask students to pay more. The state sets the boundary conditions for higher education providers. And public institutions have come under immense pressure, as the recent near-death experience of Alaska University demonstrated.[15]

Resource pathways in the UK sector have been intentionally designed to force universities to park their public mission and behave like multinational enterprises, competing for students and building stern management hierarchies accordingly. The 1997 Dearing Report and then the Browne Review in 2010 basically privatised government spending via the student loans system. Taxpayer subsidies were converted into individual interest-bearing debt. The aim was to put the customer first and have universities compete for business, creating cost efficiencies and quality controls in the process. It didn't quite work out that way. This artificial market merely transformed universities into desperate cash-hunting machines. The blight of student debt has steadily grown as a result. According to governmental reports, loans increased from just under £6 billion in 2012 to £15 billion in 2018 and are expected to reach £20 billion in 2023.[16] Higher education was essentially financialised by these policies, reflecting the UK's weird and irrational love of credit cards.

The same has happened in the US, albeit complicated by private colleges (most of which are nonprofits or '501(c)(3) Organizations', including the Ivy League) and for-profit universities. But three quarters of American students still attend public institutions, with state governments bankrolling most of the operating costs. Between 1990 and 2010 funding for full-time enrolled students in public universities dropped by 26 per cent.[17] During the same period tuition fees rose by 113 per cent as universities charged students to make up the shortfall. The rivalry for international students is now fierce. As one commentator put it, most universities have 'moved away from working to educate people in their region to competing for the most elite and wealthy students – in a way that was unprecedented'.[18] For the not-so-wealthy, student debt is an inevitable corollary. It is expected to reach US$2 trillion by 2022, larger than credit card debt and auto-loans.[19] In light of the massive economic downturn caused by the Covid-19 pandemic, the human costs of educational debt – including suicide and severe economic hardship – are only set to escalate.

US universities also spend a good part of their budgets on non-teaching/non-research managerial staff, a trend that has been replicated in other countries. In many institutions, bureaucrats now outnumber faculty and have seen a steady increase in salaries.[20] Personnel surrounding Vice Chancellors and Presidents have conspicuously ballooned. This has been driven by deregulated fees (an influx of debt-enabled cash) and universities resorting to command and control to have researchers crank out more publications and research grants, particularly since adjuncts do most of the teaching, whom likewise attract a sprawling cadre of supervisors.[21]

4.

Returning to my point, one cannot contest the neoliberal university without considering wider networks of governmentality and thus broadening our analysis to unwieldly levels. This often acrimonious government-university relationship muddies the waters further. For instance, it's easy to find senior university representatives whom seem contrite and progressive, nothing like the market-fanatics one might presume heading these organisations. But that's not the point. Indeed, a healthy dose of scepticism about commercialisation among executives may help *facilitate* the corporatisation process: 'I don't like this more than anyone else, but we have no choice.' On some occasions this subjective disidentification with neoliberalism can run down the entire management hierarchy, including individual schools, centres and departments, creating a double life for personnel; harsh technocracy at the coalface on the one hand and a culture of left-leaning complaint on the other, where junior staff and Associate Deans bemoan the draconian trends afoot as they enact them anyway.

With the university being monetised in this invidious fashion, wider socio-economic class divisions make a predictable comeback. The post-World War II university was somewhat of an aberration in this respect. The concept of 'free' higher education (i.e., government subsidised via a progressive taxation system) and its democratisation was partially an offshoot of the labour-capital compact. The war and its class dynamics meant that potential mass unrest was a genuine threat to the elite. Returning soldiers weren't simply going to slot back into their downtrodden roles. But time passes and memories fade. The corporate university was haphazardly constructed on the hoof and represents a throwback to an earlier ideal of economic privilege, where independent wealth is necessary to enjoy its rewards. That many of the politicians who champion these market reforms were themselves beneficiaries of free education is an irony that's touched upon throughout this book.

We witnessed the implications of this brazen financialisation with the US college admissions scandal in 2019, which embroiled

Desperate Housewives star Felicity Huffman and Lori Loughlin from *Full House*. If the underlying message is that affluence determines the new rules of the game, it isn't long before unscrupulous individuals vie for an unfair advantage and merit falls to the wayside. In 2011 William Rick Singer set up a coaching charity promising to give prospective students (and their parents) 'the key' to Ivy League colleges. It was in fact a sophisticated fraud operation that reached deep into a number of major universities, including Stanford, UCLA and Yale. Investigators discovered that parents paid Singer considerable sums to have their children's SAT scores falsified (often using stand-ins), bribe college officials (including testimonies about athletic ability and faked photos showing applicants playing sports, etc.) and other acts of corruption.

The scandal was reported to the public as a rare exception, bad apples that don't reflect the norm. Meritocracy and equal access continue to prevail. Yet one might also argue that the scandal merely represents an illegitimate version of what the system already achieves through otherwise 'legitimate' means.[22] Is it really a coincidence that kids from rich families disproportionately (by a staggering margin) end up at Harvard, Oxford, MIT, Cambridge and Stanford?[23] Indeed, former US President George W. Bush, a man not renowned for his sharp intellect, summed up the situation perfectly while addressing Yale Grad students about his time there: 'if you're like me, you won't remember everything you did here', referring to his legendary partying. As for his infamous verbal gaffes, Bush said, 'everything I know about the spoken word, I learned right here at Yale'.[24]

Given the brief semi-democratisation of university education during the heyday of Keynesianism, the return to a private-orientated approach needed a transitory period, of which we are entering the concluding phase. Student loans in the US, UK, Australasia and elsewhere sought to retain the 'access to all' precept, while consolidating the exact opposite behind the scenes.

Meanwhile, commercialisation has had a depressing impact on the experience of study in the neoliberal university. A major theme in this book is the emotional injuries that dark academia exact upon students too, who are often missing in arguments about the fall of the faculty. Economic pressures from both inside the higher education-complex and beyond, including the broader cost of living crisis, has made learning a traumatic endeavour; at least for those without rich parents.

Most students cope and are quietly forgotten. However, burnout, economic distress and suicide is the university's dirty little secret today. Desperate conditions provoke desperate behaviour. An undergrad at France's Lyon 2 made this clear in November 2019 when he set himself on fire outside the university ministry building. We only know him as Anas K. The 22-year-old announced on Facebook prior to the incident, 'I accuse Macron, Hollande, Sarkozy and the European Union of killing me by creating uncertainty over everyone's futures.'[25] His living allowance had been axed and he dwelt in slum-like conditions, 'with cockroaches, bedbugs and humidity'. Anas K. received serious burns to 90 per cent of his body. Student activists highlighted that 20 per cent of French students live below the poverty line and one third go without medical care. In short, they're being privatised to death, a process closely linked to deteriorating conditions for lecturers and tutors too.

5.

To simplify matters, I think four major historical shifts have occurred when it comes to shaping the *raison d'être* of the modern university, in the Western world at least.

The first took place towards the beginning of the Late Modern period. The Humboldtian breakthrough accomplished the unthinkable and placed critical and civic reason at the heart of higher education, triggering a major break with various ecclesiastical antecedents.[26] While still rivalled by older models – particularly the archaic *grandes écoles* in France – the Humboldtian university soon became very influential. But it was still an elitist institution, dominated by white male privilege, plutocratic preferentiality and strange roles like *Privatdozent*, where junior staff had to ask students for payment.[27] By the early twentieth century the US liberal university superseded these European approaches, paving the way for significant changes like actually paying early career academics![28]

Second comes the mid-twentieth century transformation, the so-called *academic revolution*.[29] Higher education was on the brink of democratisation and humanism came to the fore within the scholarly and student community. Universities were soon an echo chamber for the radical contradictions of capitalism more widely as a result of this socialisation. The massification that ensued should've been an emancipatory moment in higher education but was soon seized upon by the New Right. For example, the 1963 Robbins Report in the UK recommended that higher education degrees 'should be available to all who are qualified for them by ability and attainment', which saw a large expansion in student numbers.[30] This sounds great. But we should also remember that the report's author, Lord Robbins, was an ardent devotee of F.A. Hayek, whom he recruited while director at the London School of Economics. That a sizable price tag was eventually placed on these degrees, spawning a mega-industrial complex in its turn, isn't too surprising.

This brings us to the third shift, the counter-revolution following the birth of neoliberalism in the UK, US, New Zealand and Europe. From the mid-1980s onwards, definitive Keynesian-era public institutions were thoughtlessly commercialised, either sold off or legally mandated to behave (and compete for funds) like private business firms. The infamous 1985 Jarratt Report recommended UK universities abandon consensus-style governance methods and replace them with executive authority, top-down management and performance metrics ... lots of metrics. In Australia the Dawkins Reforms did the same. The Todd report was New Zealand's equivalent and so on.

Modern universities initially fell back on their rich historical roots to fend off the nastiest excesses of this marketisation process, but only for so long. Tuition fees, league tables and big management soon took over. Academics were recast as course delivery workers and outranked by non-academic managers. Students were defined as future employees who required training, which was priced at the market rate accordingly. Then came the considerable inroads that private enterprise made into higher education, converting innumerable science and engineering departments into proxy R&D hubs for the biomedical and defence industries.[31]

By and large, these major shifts in higher education came as a blow to academics. As analyst Ruth Barcan puts it, if scholars once considered their vocation a lifelong labour of love then the sentiment is no longer being reciprocated by employers.[32] Loving what you do is great but unrequited love is depressing.

Trends set into motion during this period were nearing their zenith when the 2020 Coronavirus pandemic struck. Things might have been bad, but clearly the worst was yet to come. That's our fourth transformation, the full implications of which we're only beginning to appreciate. Beleaguered by managerial-bloat, business bullshit and a Covid-compromised economic environment, the idea of the modern university may soon be coming to an end. My examination of dark academia isn't just an economic story, however. You won't find any statistical tables and graphs about funding streams and debt cycles, since these are available elsewhere. Instead I want to scrutinise what those objective structures do to students and academics on a subjective level. This story regrettably involves the usual litany of maladies associated with extreme capitalism as it careens towards the abyss: suicide, self-harm, depression, chronic stress and anxiety. So I duly warn readers that the following analysis may be rather alarming.

2.

La La Land

1.

In their bleak synopsis of the corporate university, Nick Lewis and Cris Shore describe a faraway world called 'Faculty Land'.[1] The term was mentioned by senior administrators when describing academics, a snarky derivative of *Fantasyland* from Disney World.

Inhabitants of Faculty Land are blissfully unaware of the real-world pressures that most people face. Protected in their intellectual cocoons, academics are far removed from the average taxpaying citizen who ends up paying for this indulgence. It's easy to imagine the Trump-like tone these administrators adopt as they mock Faculty Land once again: those snobs don't realise how good they've got it ... and we pay for it! No more! No more!

Variants of this narrative persist in popular culture too, although not always as facetious. Many people still believe that scholars lead a decidedly privileged existence, leisurely writing books, discussing esoteric topics in tweed jackets and sipping brandy in the evening as they contemplate complex problems. Academia is considered an abstruse, yet gilded occupation. Whatever professors do in those ivory towers, they certainly have little to complain about, a conclusion that unfortunately resonates in these anti-intellectual times.[2]

The contradiction between this dreamy picture of scholarly life and the dark reality wreaking havoc in universities today remains pervasive, even as the Covid-19 crisis summarily crushes the profession before our eyes ('what are they doing with all that free time at home?'). For several years critical university studies has tried to change this perception, including Bill Readings's seminal *The University in Ruins* and Benjamin Ginsberg's *The Fall of the Faculty*.[3] But it hasn't greatly altered the idealised view of Faculty Land and people are still incredulous when you tell them what it's really like. What? You have a line-manager setting strict performance targets and threatening to terminate your position if you don't comply? You work how many hours a week? That can't be!

Most critical investigations of the corporate university tend to focus on the structural transformations that have occurred over the past 35 years.[4] Frustrating and sometimes schizophrenic institutions have emerged from these market-led reforms, resulting in what Richard Hill amusingly calls 'whackademia'.[5] Impenetrable levels of bureaucracy. The extraordinary growth of managers and administrators. First come Deans. Then Associate Deans. Assistant Associate Deans after that. And finally Senior Assistant Associate Deans to round it off. CEO-like leaders enjoying staggering salaries and travelling the globe. The dubious use of insecure contracts. Glitzy ad campaigns that cost a fortune.

And let's not forget a teaching approach that resembles industrial mass-production.

When it comes to understanding how these *objective* changes in universities affect its workforce on a *subjective* (even unconscious) level, my argument is simple. If large formal institutions encourage certain types of selfhood, a rudimentary insight of organisational sociology, then higher education today is undoubtedly producing damaged people. Don't believe the hype in those sleek university brochures. Stress, chronic fatigue, depression and suicide ideation are endemic. Indeed, the evidence now coming to light on this topic makes for grim reading, even before the 2020 pandemic made the situation much worse.

2.

The term 'neoliberalism' is way overused, of course, almost a cliché. It's ascribed to anything negatively associated with contemporary capitalism.[6] And since some suggest its star may now be fading after the turn to ethno-nationalism in the West, I evoke it with some hesitation. But even if the ideology is in decline (which is debateable), its effects are writ large across higher education in many respects. Neoliberalism essentially refers to radical changes in the way governments organise the economy, with special priority given to private enterprise (including its memetic forms in the public sector) and expansive financialisation.[7] That's a pretty simplistic definition now that its international manifestation (e.g., globalisation) is reverting into a sort of 'national neoliberalism'.[8] And during the Coronavirus pandemic, it became evident that this economic model was unable to reproduce its own axiomatic principles. The demise of many higher education institutions is now a real possibility.

The tremendous commercialisation of universities – particularly those in the public sphere – has had major consequences. These institutions are now fees-driven, with funding structures designed to render them more competitive. As such, many universities treat themselves as large business concerns, with highflying CEOs (Vice Chancellors and Presidents who are typically suited men) and strident management hierarchies now dominating them. Managerialism has created a massive division between value-adding staff and authority. It's not uncommon for academics to be supervised by managers who've never published a journal article or taught a large undergraduate class.[9] They demand compliance because the university is viewed as a *technical* problem first and foremost. And performance metrics are their weapon of choice.

Why is it when you speak to any academic at the moment – from mathematicians and dramatists to musculoskeletal biologists and medieval philosophers – their main grievance, the one that keeps them up at night, is university management? Universities have always had hierarchies, of course. But today they adopt a specific tone, a barely masked antipathy that shuns discussion and open dialogue. In turn, this has fostered what I call 'the great divide' in higher education: the gulf between those who manage and those who teach/research. These two domains are pretty much worlds apart now. How many academics today think of their Dean and President as 'colleagues' instead of bosses? Very few. This unusual state of affairs is so taken for granted that it's not questioned anymore.

Enhanced efficiency is a stock justification for technocracy in contemporary universities.[10] But what's considered 'efficient' is in the eye of the beholder. For administrators, Office 365 is ideal for firing off various demands, especially if fully automated. Whereas email is the antitheses of efficiency for faculty bogged down by endless requests. Growing student admissions and filling lecture halls to overcapacity is an efficient method for increasing revenue. For teachers who deliver the classes, it's a massive pain in the arse. Creating an elaborate audit trail for expense reimbursements permits the university to efficiently monitor spending. For academics it becomes a time-consuming and tortuous exercise.

When the 2020 Coronavirus crisis unfolded, transferring classes online in a speedy manner was the most efficient way to retain student enrolments. For teaching staff it meant an inordinate amount of work, much of which was done in the evenings and weekends, carrying substantial hidden costs. Internet breaks down at home? That's your personal problem, not the university's, so fix it ... or else!

In any case, this is precisely why some senior managers may believe their school/department is running like clockwork, whereas faculty experience wild and boundless confusion. Add a touch of authoritarianism to the mix and these work environments can easily turn bad.

3.

The negative fallout associated with this conversion of universities into commoditised production-lines is increasingly difficult to ignore. Let's first consider undergraduate students. Are they really an ungrateful generation of 'snowflakes' who don't know how good they have it?[11] Hardly. In today's environment, they represent a major source of revenue and are put to work. With funding cuts and austerity being the guiding policy of governments over the last two decades, cramming lecture halls is now essential best practice for universities.[12] Bums on seats is the underlying motto, even if this is done virtually as transpired during the Coronavirus catastrophe.

So how have students fared in an environment that's more intense than ever before?

Sophisticated studies can now isolate university life as an independent variable when examining the distribution of psychological morbidity within the student population (e.g., did enrolling in higher education increase a student's experience of mental illness 'to a significant degree', etc.).[13] The findings are disconcerting. In a global investigation of 14,000 students in 19 countries, researchers found that 35 per cent experienced (at least) one of six mental health disorders noted in the *Diagnostic and Statistical Manual of Mental Disorders*.[14] Contributing factors included demanding workloads, the pressure to excel and financial worries.

Incidences of campus self-harm and attempted suicide no longer surprise fellow students. For example, after 13 student suicides at Bristol University over a short period, an undergrad was asked about how it affected him: 'if I sound unfazed by the suicides, it's because it's happened so much since first year. As awful as it is, I'm used to it and have sort of become desensitised.'[15] Bristol University officials are now so desperate that they recently implemented a 'Fitness to Study' policy, suspending at-risk students and removing them from classes. For Ruth Day, being sent home and barred from campus, 'left me trying to deal with weeks of having a huge question mark hanging over my future, feeling uncertain and lost, with no mental health support at all'.[16] Ironically, a policy designed to assist troubled students was instead experienced as exclusionary and exacerbated their anguish.

Undergrads in the US too have seen an increase in the prevalence of suicidal thoughts, depression and incapacitating anxiety. Researchers recently examined two sets of data tracking mental wellbeing in higher education, one including 610,000 undergraduates between 2011 and 2018 and the other 177,000 students between 2007 and 2018.[17] Suicide attempts rose from 0.7 per cent in 2013 to 1.8 per cent in 2018. Students reporting depression jumped from 9.4 per cent to 21.1 per cent. No wonder more parents are filing class action lawsuits against colleges, claiming they've failed their duty of care. In the case of Olivia Kong, an undergraduate at the University of Pennsylvania, campus counsellors were notified several times about her suicidal bouts. Kong said she hated herself for falling behind in school. Following one phone call with the distressed undergraduate, a university psychiatrist merely noted: 'said that she had actually planned to return to campus Sunday and kill herself'.[18] And she did.

Grad students – undertaking masters and doctoral studies – are facing similar mental health problems. A 2018 study of 2279 postgraduate students in 26 countries found 40 per cent had suffered moderate/severe depression and anxiety, six times higher than in the population at large.[19] *Nature* followed up on these findings by inviting students to share their reasons why. A research fellow at Imperial College blamed the competitive environment for his troubles: 'the research culture lies at the core of many scientists' mental-health issues. The environment is hyper-competitive, and the path for success is almost impossibly narrow. That's a scenario that breeds anxiety and depression … It is a situation where everyone is pursuing a goal that's almost impossible to reach.'[20]

Hyper-competitive careerism is a cornerstone of the neoliberal university and future employment prospects have a big influence on graduate wellbeing.[21] Metrics, grants and top-tier publications now function as performance indicators for distributing the best jobs in a tight labour market that has radically shrunk following the global pandemic. But competitiveness is notoriously erosive, frequently inducing fear of failure. The problem is that higher education now pivots on this very principle and the toll it inflicts has been largely ignored until recently. Moreover, it's important to note that many grad students today also work as seasonal lecturers, lab demonstrators and research assistants. Unlike the archetypical student qua passive consumer, they can also be classified as workers or producers and thus inhabit an undesirable liminal space.[22]

4.

How bad is it now to work as an academic in the contemporary university? According to a recent YouGov survey of UK lecturers, 55 per cent said they felt exceptionally stressed and mentally unwell.[23] Causes were said to be mandatory changes by management without consultation, unrealistic workloads (affecting work/life balance) and lack of time for proper research.

The report noted that academics are working longer hours, becoming increasing isolated and stuck on a 'treadmill of justification' where proving one's worth to superiors is never-ending. The highly disorganised and obtuse nature of this managerialism compounds the problem. As one stressed-out lecturer remarked, 'I felt whatever I put work into I would be blamed for what I wasn't doing. The system feels chaotic and you don't understand how you're being judged.'[24]

Scholars are extremely self-motivated and have always been prone to overwork. Since most are driven by an intrinsic commitment to their vocation, it can be difficult to switch off after hours. I know plenty of academics for whom nothing is more relaxing than holidaying on the beach with a dense monograph. But the workaholicism afflicting universities today is different. It's not voluntary but linked to externally imposed demands on our time, something that the recent Covid-19 crisis raised to new heights. In many cases, lecturers are tacitly expected to overperform in all parts of their job like some modern day *uomo universal*, excelling in teaching, publishing, research grants, administrative service, public engagement and so forth. That they are subsequently overwhelmed, both mentally and physically, is to be expected, with burnout an endemic occupational hazard, exacerbated by unhealthy lifestyles and unhappy relationships.[25]

Part of the problem is the way higher education institutions relate with each other in the marketplace. The ubiquitous use of 'benchmarking' (which business firms have long criticised) is a case in point. It provides the perfect pretext for near unachievable performance goals.[26] Low-tier and mid-tier universities are optimistically calibrated to 'top five' institutions, minus the abundant resources and generous endowments, of course: 'we must be ambitious!' faculty are told, usually via a mass-recipient email. However, benchmarking not only generates unthinking isomorphism or copying other universities for its own sake. According to analyst Liz Morrish, it also transforms workplaces into dangerous 'anxiety machines' because expectations are *never* dialled down, only up.[27] This could be why academic counselling referrals have increased by 73 per cent in the last ten years in UK universities.[28] At some institutions the figure was 300 per cent. Despite the colourful staff wellbeing programmes that the neoliberal university adores to advertise, senior officials still refuse to address the underlying factors that are fuelling mental illness in academia.[29]

Unpaid overtime is yet another sign of this anxiety machine. In England, one study found that academics regularly work two unpaid days per week, with professors working on average 56.1 hours per week and principal research fellows 55.7 hours. One in six academics under the age of 25 work 100 hours per week. Overall the findings stressed how 'unreasonable, unsafe and excessive hours' has become in UK higher education.[30] Cynics might respond that the above figures exaggerate the real situation, a product of liberal self-reporting. Before jumping to that conclusion, take a look at Queen Mary University of London. Overworked staff were warned by executive management that if they continued to sleep in their offices disciplinary action would be forthwith. A professor at the university remarked,

> there is a problem with overwork among academics, but it's difficult to talk about because of the popular impression that we get paid very well for doing not that much ... academics can end up spending an awful lot of their so-called free time actually doing work.[31]

The UK is not an outlier. Remarkably similar trends have been documented in other countries that have corporatised tertiary education. This is particularly evident with the growth of insecure contracts, which are now pervasive in the Edu-Factory. Whereas managerialism turns the screw on full-time academics by increasing their workload, casual adjuncts have economic precarity added to the equation. In the US, they have significantly changed the composition of the academic labour market and frequently outnumber tenured staff.[32] The psychological strain suffered by this academic underclass, whose plight has been recently high-lighted by several shocking deaths, ought to be centre-stage in any attempt to exorcise the phantom of managerialism from the university today.[33]

5.

The art of teaching noticeably changes under these conditions. For some reason, few in the neoliberal university are willing to admit that lecturing and tutoring is *difficult*. To do it well takes a great deal of work and preparation. Only after years of practice, figuring out what works and what doesn't, does it become fluid and truly scholastic. This is why teaching in the corporate university can be profoundly disheartening.

Oliver Lee, a US historian, recounts the moment he decided to quit his well-paid job and do something completely different.[34] Everything was going well until the dream slowly unravelled: 'first there was sniping, from peers and administrators'. Sadly, this – including gossip and backstabbing – is common in academia today given the aggressive careerism that's encouraged. But then Lee mentions teaching. He was getting some excellent student evaluations, which management looked upon with suspicion, as if he was somehow cheating the system. Then one day a buddy dropped by to see him in action. The friend said afterwards it was difficult to concentrate due to the student sitting in front of him. Lee explains: 'that student, who like all in-state students was paying $50 per lecture to hear me talk, was watching season one of *Breaking Bad*. In a class with no attendance grade, where the lectures were at least halfway decent, he was watching *Breaking Bad*.'[35]

In a perverse way, perhaps this represents a neoliberal inversion of the transgressive moment black feminist bell hooks once advocated apropos the emancipated university.[36] Not a freedom that springs from a radical engagement with texts, but a radical dis-engagement with pedagogy itself. Now that students have paid for admission, as far as the university is concerned, they've already fulfilled their half of the bargain. Adding insult to injury, it's entirely possible that our *Breaking Bad* fan might still complain about their final grade, perhaps writing an angry email demanding special consideration.

The story is certainly demoralising. But it makes little sense blaming students. Their behaviour reflects the institutional matrix in which they study. As Kevin Gannon recently observed, if it's never been more difficult to teach in higher education than in the present moment then exactly the same applies to learning.[37] Covid-19 simply accentuated these dynamics, shifting them online and into academic households for one long hellish year.

The way international students are treated is indicative of this industrial teaching ethos. They frequently make up a significant proportion of enrolments in many institutions and cash-flow depends on signing up more kids. Consequently, it's been alleged that some universities turn a blind eye to English language standards to get more through the door. Once in the classroom, learning becomes a painful and disorientating exercise.

In 2019 an Australian mathematics lecturer – Dr Gerd Schröder-Turk – explained the problem on primetime television, naming his own university in the process.[38] That was a big mistake. Senior management were furious and threatened to sue him for millions, claiming that Schröder-Turk had traduced the university and breached his fiduciary duties. The intimidation seemed excessive, but perhaps that was the point. A warning to others about speaking out. That international students in Australia find life very difficult is probably connected to all this. In the Australian state of Victoria, for example, at least 27 international students committed suicide between 2009 and 2015.[39]

6.

The economic rationalisation of higher education hasn't entirely been one-way traffic. As I argued earlier, it would be very tempting to tell a story of academics being forced to accept this new regime. But as Mike Marinetto recently observed, we've played our own part in creating this scenario, gaming the system for career advancement and endowing leading journals with near quasi-religious powers.[40] In the US, UK and Australia, for instance, promotion and salaries have been narrowly tallied to the number of 'top' publications you possess. Playing the game has become an open secret and the professional rewards are significant, which are inversely proportional to the retributions meted out if one doesn't join in.

The corporate university has cunningly interwoven rational self-interest (a hallmark of neoclassical economics that emphasises utility maximisation) with our vocational love for reading and writing, qualities that intrinsically motivate academics. Sometimes it's difficult to tell whether the reason we're working so hard is due to our 'calling' or because management incentive systems demand it. Realising it's largely been the latter has tainted something important in the profession, with ambition and celebrity culture displacing core scholastic values. Making matters worse, academics made another stupid mistake. They reinterpreted occupational autonomy and freedom through the prism of individualism – being left alone and detached from organisational responsibilities – rather than collegial self-governance.[41] An army of bureaucrats were waiting to fill the vacuum. Now they pretty much run universities.

Yet another headwind we face relates to the title of this chapter, the perpetuation of an image of academics as snobbish elites who have their heads in the clouds. Hardline conservatives and libertarians love espousing the mythos of La La Land. Weirdly, students too are included in this misleading ascription. According to Greg Lukianoff and Jonathan Haidt's *The Coddling of the American Mind*, college students are suffering from precisely the opposite problem to the one argued in this book: they're being treated with kid gloves and pampered like fragile flowers.[42] They need to harden up! Amazingly, the book was a runaway success, which tells us about the mentality we're up against.

So what is to be done? There is no easy answer. Modern universities have long reflected the wider political climate in which they exist, especially government policy. But if they are to become human-centric spaces again, the dominant managerial approach must be rolled back. Academic despair is simply a reasonable response to these alienating conditions. Out of necessity, many bunker down and try to make the best of a bad situation.[43] Mortgages have to be paid after all. But this heightens the isolation and inner turmoil. Professional solidarity soon breaks down. Some academics can go for weeks or even months without seeing each other as they frenetically type away at home.

Collective self-recovery must supersede this 'survival mode' strategy. It is almost too simple to list the changes that could be made in this respect, even at a school or departmental level: participatory budgeting; collective deliberation on new appointments; staff electing academics to senior positions, with candidates outlining their plans in advance (and making them recallable); the school's mission being extensively debated, and only then carried to the university level; students having more meaningful input than simply rating the popularity of lecturers; the eradication of casual contracts; and most importantly, rejecting the blind fetishisation of efficiency.

As Stefano Harney and Fred Moten remark, academia must be de-colonised from the *inside* out.[44] Power hasn't just got us by our pay check but also the subjective templates we use to make sense of the profession. Thus a renewed conception of what scholarship and pedagogy really means is essential, once the journal ranking lists and Student Feedback Survey scores have been abandoned. If we aren't simply production-line knowledge workers imparting practical skills for the capitalist labour market ... then what are we? Answering that question is invariably tied to broader political problems connected to the nation-state, which too is in crisis. And progressive change at that level is unlikely in the near future. In the meantime, the university slowly wilts on the inside.

3

Welcome to the Edu-Factory

1.

Although it was supposed to be a faculty 'Away Day', we were sitting in a room only a few hundred metres from the university. Budgets were tight and departmental austerity was in full bloom. The Dean took centre-stage and gave a talk largely consisting of corporate buzzword phrases: 'significant stretch targets'; 'get our friends in the tent'; 'the aha effect'; 'global mindset'; 'clean up the box we live in'; 'big buckets you then sharpen'.

A bewildered colleague beside me leant in and whispered, 'these Away Days are so bloody depressing'. I nodded in agreement, mirroring the forlorn faces around me. But worse was to come. Next on the agenda was a team building exercise involving African drumming. As we banged away on our cheap djembes in embarrassment, the Dean was nowhere to be seen. Exhausted, tyrannised by office email and under pressure to meet performance targets, the Away Day felt like some kind of cruel joke.

The restructuring of the university into a knowledge factory – where academic expertise is tightly controlled via performance metrics, key performance indicators (KPIs) and an all-encompassing emphasis on processing ever more students – has revolutionised the tertiary education sector.[1] Departments and schools across the university have been forced to undergo this corporate metamorphosis. Social work and medicine, physics and astronomy, the biological sciences, engineering, philosophy, law and economics, to name only a few, are now meant to behave like independent business units; that is to say, compete for resources from central administration, attract external income (from industry, etc.) and grow student enrolments. When first introduced this was called a 'cost recovery' model and fiscal sustainability was the rationale. But today *surpluses* are expected. If a school or department fails to add to the university's bottom-line then serious questions are soon asked about its future viability.

The mantra of 'business relevance' has rapidly advanced this process. Universities must now demonstrate wider societal impact and justify how its activities contribute to innovation and economic vibrancy. Industry partnerships with big business naturally follow, commoditising knowledge (patents, intellectual property, etc.) and seriously undermining the public spirit of higher education.[2] Capitalising on discoveries and making cash from them is now a major driver of inquiry, not the betterment of humanity. Related to this is the legitimacy of postgraduate programmes. Their validity hinges on future employability prospects rather than the inherent quality of the curriculum. Hence the disproportionate importance placed on STEM subjects (Science, Technology, Engineering and Mathematics) compared to other disciplines, with the humanities the clear loser as it withers on the vine.[3] In short, universities must prove themselves as servants to the cult of work, well-functioning job factories that invariably charge students a small fortune for the privilege. But what kind of jobs await?

2.

The businessification of universities parallels the neoliberalisation of society more generally. Although its origins stretch back to policy decisions in the 1980s, some of the most decisive changes occurred in the 1990s. This is when the battle was effectively lost and higher education was revamped as an industrial-complex. Mass degree production became a leading export sector in many countries, manufacturing students, journal publications and assorted 'outputs', all monitored with factory-like accounting analytics.

As with other big corporations, a roseate storyline has been simultaneously evoked to soften the hard edges, especially in larger public universities that desire to be construed in a virtuous light: 'R U OK Day' and warm wellbeing programmes are celebrated by HR; environmental sustainability and cultural diversity are proudly sponsored by leaders; prominent charities are endorsed; empty management buzzwords and euphemisms replace ordinary communication – all of which sits beside a disciplinary power structure that's ready to pounce if anyone steps out of line.

The business bullshit (including African drumming exercises) described in the opening real-life experience does not contradict the combative technocracy currently prevailing in higher education but *supplements* it. That this New Agey babble appears only *after* capitalist realism has conquered the university is no coincidence. Faculty would have considered 'Employee

Assistance Programmes' and 'Vice Chancellor consultation clinics' decidedly alien prior to the managerialisation of their workplaces. If there is no iron-fist, then why bother with the velvet glove? That's when a significant inversion takes place, with scholarly curiosity and patient study looking decidedly alien instead. Inside the Edu-Factory, academics often feel strangers to the vocation they've given most of their adult lives to. The disparity is imperative: it's a clash between the intrinsic reasons why many became academics in the first place and powerful institutional efforts to reinvent higher education as a business enterprise not dissimilar to News Corp.[4]

Why does this tension matter? Well, like other 'deep vocations' that are primarily motivated by the craft itself, the job often goes to the heart of who academics are as individuals. Pay and conditions are important, of course, but few begin their careers with the goal of getting rich or becoming famous. A quantum engineer or legal historian spends years studying his or her chosen field, mostly outside of office hours, because they are completely absorbed by the basic problems it poses. Much of the time they see little difference between themselves and what they do for a living. This unique facet of the profession often chimes with a wider sense of civic duty too – *veritas cum libertate* – like furthering public knowledge and societal progress.[5]

All of this is wonderful if the job is going well. But what happens when a semi-hostile management matrix begins to surround you from all sides? Students demanding better grades from *below*, competitive co-workers closing in from the *side*, petty bureaucrats *above* ... not to mention senior executives from *high above* whom are seldom seen in person. Emails around the clock. The academic calling is dismantled brick by brick. Slowly the miasma gets under the skin. And because scholars are trained to study important phenomenon closely, they begin to study *that* too ... with dark intensity.

3.

More specifically, the Edu-Factory is the product of several forces that are ongoing and by no means settled. But commercialisation is central.[6] In the public education sector, the urgency placed on financial accountability and market competitiveness by government policymakers jolted the university into a new worldview concerning its organisational mission. Starving institutions of proper funding compelled them to compete for students in a global marketplace, overhauling their management structures *as if* they were corporations. A complicated corporation to be sure, since most universities are nonprofits and charities. This is significant because organisations mandated by public purpose goals ought to follow very different governance patterns compared to for-profit businesses.[7] When universities emulate corporations, therefore, the incompatibilities between the two logics permits a kind of bad faith to develop. On the one hand, institutions profess their community agenda, as most nonprofits do. Whereas on the other, KPIs, capital deferral instruments and labour cost reduction strategies completely preoccupy management and their phalanx of functionaries.

Accountants and their attendant vocabulary dominate this realm. Questions about academic integrity or the ethical responsibilities of public education, for example, are the last things being discussed in the university C-suite. Instead a razor-thin financial prerogative controls the conversation because institutions either sink or swim on the basis of future earnings. This financialisation has seeped into the very texture of higher education. When the Covid-19 pandemic hit in March 2020 the only thing staff talked about – from the top of the hierarchy to the bottom – were the economic implications. Revenue, income and fiscal viability had so utterly seized our political imaginations. Even unions couldn't escape this insidious framework. Money was the only factor that really mattered – *facta bruta* – which is an *ideological* achievement as much as an economic one.

This keys into a deceptive discourse of *economic realism*, which preaches 'living within our means' as opposed to the unsustainable, unrealistic and utopian alternatives presented on the left. Economic realism looks neutral and objective, like sober advice of an accountant, but that's misleading. For example, the post-Coronavirus job losses (and budget cuts) were justified in the name of prudent and sustainable fiscal management. Look at the numbers, there's no alternative! But I don't remember many university leaders talking about 'sustainability' prior to the pandemic when institutions were raking in millions from the international student market model, one that commentators warned was unsustainable for years. And why wasn't a portion of these huge surpluses put aside as a safety buffer against unforeseen downturns in the market, as is standard practice in industry? Furthermore, rather than firing staff off the bat, interest-free loans could have tided universities over during the recovery period. In other words, there are alternatives because economic decisions are always based on a set of underlying values. Nevertheless, this economic realism has been very difficult to call into question.

The marketisation of higher education functions (or malfunctions depending on whom you ask) in another way, by exploiting the age-old teacher/student relationship in a stealthy fashion. After purchasing the advertised services from the brochure, the student-consumer is nominally 'empowered'. They expect good grades and a well-paying job no matter what. This not only changes the relationship between teachers and students, but also academics and administrators. Given that customer satisfaction is essential, professional services staff invariably switch into de facto supervisors, sending a raft of demands, requests and requirements with firm deadlines. As previously remarked, good management is difficult. You have to engage with your people and be collegial, so senior administrators opt for the carrot-and-stick formula instead, deploying performance management systems that wouldn't be out of place in KMPG.[8]

When worried observers warn that the public university is nearing death, what they really mean is its once resilient *counter-business* ethos, something that right-wing governments have sought to stamp out for years.[9] They hated the idea that we study medieval poetry not because of graduate employability prospects but because it's the right thing to do. That we study the metastasis of colon cancer not because lucrative licensing payments await, but because it's the right thing to do. The neoliberal university has abjured its identification with *res publica* so resoundingly. Academic praxis is now about obedience to bureaucratic authority and adding to the institution's financial prosperity. Hence why many feel like overworked subcontractors rather than public educators dedicated to advancing human knowledge and cultural progress.

4.

A significant catalyst for these changes was the introduction of New Public Management (or NPM) into state services. The bastard child of public sector reforms during the Thatcher and Reagan era, it reflected the New Right's animus towards so-called 'big government'.[10] At face value, NPM could be defined as the use of mental models from the business world to run public organisations. But it's more iniquitous than that. NPM manipulates the notion of 'public interest' to its own advantage, erroneously picturing it as an irate taxpayer who thinks academics have been freeriding far too long. Tenured professors should especially be given a good kick up the arse and taught a lesson about working in the real world. It's time to wake up Prof! Unfortunately, this wake-up call has been continuing for several decades now, grinding down faculty (including junior lecturers and adjuncts) into cowering shadows of their former selves.

The hypothetical aim of NPM was to make universities, hospitals, kindergartens and public broadcasters more cost-effective and transparent to taxpayers. Hence the massive reliance on accounting metrics linked to this governance method. Unofficially, however, NPM represents a dirty war on the public sphere, including its powerful (then at least) workers' unions. NPM gains inspiration from neoclassical economics, including more aggressive variants like Public Choice Theory, popularised by James M. Buchanan.[11] It presents an ultra-cynical view of government and state services. Public servants operate behind a veil of municipal duty. But in reality they're selfish opportunists like everyone else and will try to maximise their narrow interests at the taxpayers' expense. Public institutions should be administered with this assumption in mind and establish stern controls that promise fiscal accountability, individual performance targets and lean spending strategies.

Look, I'm not going to romanticise the situation. Some academics do misbehave and require a firm hand. Senior managers become visibly jaded dealing with them. But it is an entirely different matter to oversee a system that pre-emptively treats *all* faculty as if they are self-seeking chancers. That's a self-fulfilling prophesy in the making and leads to a climate of deadening control.

When NPM was discovered by modern universities, two opposing narratives weirdly coalesced, the first based on market individualism and the second gravitating towards bureaucratic collectivism. On the one hand, neoclassical economists fought long and hard to recast workers as independent and capsule-like agents. According to their mathematical theorems, 'organisations' are irrational because they shield individuals from market forces. This is when *homo economicus* or economic man comes forth. The objective was to de-collectivise the labour force and their unions. With few institutional commitments or social bonds, employers keep him or her at arm's length and allow the law of supply/

demand to manage them instead. We'll discuss the use of casuals and adjuncts shortly. But even tenured professors are encouraged to think of themselves as autonomous business owners who must attract external grants, etc.[12] On the other hand, however, NPM redefined academics as hired 'employees' rather than a community of equals. In that capacity, academics are subjected to copious levels of organisational regulation since their time now belongs to an employer who demands a certain performance.

At first glance, these two logics seem inconsistent, encouraging *both* atomised individualism and bureaucratic conformity. But the neoliberal university has somehow succeeded in concocting a potent amalgamation of both. Economic isolation and insecurity that is comingled with claustrophobic levels of performance management, corporate socialisation and close-quarters' supervision. Needless to say, this all but kills the creativity and self-determination essential to scholarly excellence and radical breakthroughs in the sciences and humanities.[13]

NPM justifies its predominance in the lingua franca of public accountability. This lends license to all kinds of invasive auditing and surveillance techniques. *Homo academicus* is now one of the most measured and audited characters in modern society! In any case, the tidal wave of numbers that track her every movement is based upon a fundamental mistake. As Cris Shore perceptively points out, 'the problem is that audit confuses "accountability" with "accountancy" so that "being answerable to the public" is recast in terms of measures of productivity, "economic efficiency" and delivering "value for money"'.[14] The spurious conflation has had ominous and enduring ramifications for the academic labour process.

5.

University management isn't new, of course. But the techniques used today mark a significant break with past governance systems.

In particular, the blending of market individualism with NPM's control-fixation and quest for cost efficiencies has irrevocably transformed the culture inside universities. For instance, it's little wonder that we are witnessing the rapid Uberfication of teaching staff.[15] Casuals and contract workers assume the role of 'ghost employees' who are technically freelancers. And like itinerant factory workers, adjuncts are paid for the exact hours they work and experience management regimes that didn't think twice about cancelling their 'gigs' during the Covid-19 pandemic.

For these reasons some have concluded that NPM is one of the crueller human inventions to emerge from the neoliberal state.[16] It combines the worst features of market insecurity and anxiety with Stalinesque levels of supervision, an imperative that public universities have honed with zest. As an employee, you might be *on your own* – in terms of economic life chances and protection – but you certainly won't be *left alone* given the incredible array of demands that will be placed on you.

Here is the strange part. Private elite institutions, including the very top-tier universities, often evince far less managerialism than state-funded ones using NPM. Compared to public universities that must justify their existence vis-à-vis an austere and hostile government, private colleges have little to prove. Admonitions about taxpayer accountability, quality assurance and transparency have been central to naturalising this new order in higher education. But in enthusiastically following this trend, some institutions have embraced the corporate mindset to unhealthy (and often unworkable) extremes. As the businessification process advances, one has to wonder whether public universities might now be *more corporate* than the archetypical corporation itself.

In order to ram through these changes, politicians and senior policy analysts disseminated a false view of pre-1980s universities, portraying them as wasteful sinkholes compared to the efficient machines before us today. I'm not sentimentalising the past by any means. Universities were never utopian paradises. But nor were they an unaccountable and profligate drain on public spending as some purport. No, the real reason that proponents of NPM mischaracterise the pre-1980s era is because higher education was then still deemed a 'common good' rather than a private commodity. Public goods are anathema to the basic values of free market capitalism. Negative caricatures of the 1960s and 1970s unfortunately continue to be employed today in order to rationalise controversial initiatives, including exorbitant fees hikes, the spread of authoritarian hierarchies, industry partnerships (with arms manufacturers and fracking firms among others) and the growth of teaching mills that worship KPIs and student numbers.[17] The irony is that universities have become top-heavy, unhappy and flabby organisations as a consequence, nothing like the agile enterprises that libertarians claim ought to exemplify the new economy.

6.

Sadly, some conservatives go even further. They're not convinced that this semi-imaginary socialist past has actually died. It is incredible that right-wing 'anti-academics' continue to complain that modern universities remain stuck in 1960s mode, hotbeds of countercultural deviance and indolence bankrolled by hardworking taxpayers. Because professors are chillaxing reading Marx and students are sucking up public money like there's no tomorrow, further reforms are required. This portrayal of colleges is certainly preposterous. But it seems to be the one that politicians are listening to, especially in the US where it's widely believed that campuses are dominated by politically correct professors who're hell bent on banning free speech.

Jason Brennan and Phillip Magness' *Cracks in the Ivory Tower* provides an excellent example of this right-wing assault in the name of market efficiency.[18] For them universities are still teeming with hippy-hugging scholars who pretend to be noble servants in pursuit of truth. But they're only out for themselves ... and usually at the institution's cost. Brennan and Magness confess that academics aren't inherently bad people, they're just like ordinary folk who want to avoid work and protect their own turf, just as Public Choice Theory predicts. The problem with modern universities thus stems from a lack of proper fiscal signals and performance metrics. In other words, academe is a textbook case of what happens when the principles of market accountability aren't in place.

The first step for shaking things up, according to Brennan and Magness, is to take a more distrustful view of those who work and study in higher education. Students are instrumentally motivated by grade point averages (GPAs) rather than learning. Administrators aim to hoard resources and have little interest in the university's wider wellbeing. But academics are the worst offenders in this respect:

> Academics often express a romantic view of academia. They believe higher education serves a number of noble purposes ... But beware. There's no guarantee that the kinds of people who want academic jobs are motivated solely or even predominately by such ideals. Sure, the kinds of people who want academic jobs may be somewhat different from the kinds of people who want to become used cars salespeople, politicians, or business executives. But people are people. Academics aren't saints.[19]

Three things come to mind regarding this argument.

First, who exactly says academics are saints? Nobody I know. This false deification of the profession is a rhetorical device, of course, a strawman that's easier to knock down.

Second, the suggestion that academics are selfishly gaming the system and can't be trusted includes anecdotes from Brennan and Magness' own activities (e.g., Jason using up research funds on needless expenses because appropriate incentive systems are not in place). Could it simply be that they are projecting their own errant tendencies onto the rest of us?

And third, one must wonder how such an extreme tract could be sanctioned by an esteemed publishing house like Oxford University Press. What were they thinking? Well ... perhaps they weren't thinking at all. Although multinational journal publishing corporations like Elsevier, Sage and Emerald have long courted controversy for extorting universities around access to their own outputs, academic monograph presses have received less attention. But some aren't much better, especially those seeking to price-gouge university library budgets with overpriced hardcovers. The business model means they'll print practically anything for a quick buck, academic capitalism in its most accelerated form.[20]

7.

With far-fetched and nasty narratives like *Cracks in the Ivory Tower* moving into the mainstream, it is little wonder that universities are busy aping the corporate world. The use of insecure and untenured labour has dramatically increased in the last two decades for this very reason. These 'flexible work systems' are not new (think of seasonal workers, for instance). But their recent encroachment into regular occupations has allowed employers to significantly cut and/or displace labour costs. Universities have predictably followed the same strategy. Herb Childress recently investigated the trend in US academia, uncovering an entire underclass of adjuncts who really do get the crappy end of the stick.[21] Today around 75 per cent of teaching staff are untenured, a massive growth in only a few years. They get paid about US$2500 per course and receive no healthcare or pension benefits. Adjuncts frequently fall below the poverty line and require welfare assistance. Sleeping in their cars and showering in college gyms isn't unheard of.[22] Hardly emblematic of the ivory tower.

At the top of the organisational apex are senior university officials who now behave more like CEOs than academics. Indeed, many come from business backgrounds and don't have doctorates, although they still claim the title of 'Professor'. Like their private sector counterparts, these executives have enjoyed exponential income growth over the last decade. Nearly half of Vice Chancellors/Presidents in the UK receive over £300,000 a year and five are paid £500,000 or more.[23] De Montfort's Vice Chancellor received a 22 per cent salary increase in 2017–18.

Most Vice Chancellors and Presidents captivated with the image of CEOs have started to use the language of corporate strategists, constructing ambitious 'strategic plans' and employing a vast number of bureaucrats to execute their vision. Large consultancy firms like EY and McKinsey have made major inroads here, quietly disseminating market logics behind the scenes. And now that universities are competing for students both locally and internationally, they need to leverage existing kudos or build brand awareness that conveys exclusivity. Showy marketing campaigns, rivalling those in big business, are today considered best practice, as expensive billboards and online ads emphasise image over substance to snare that elusive student dollar.[24]

The foray into high finance completes the corporate phantasy. Government austerity combined with the idolisation of growth (new buildings and facilities to accommodate growing student numbers, etc.) has seen debt become a major facet in university operations. As Leigh Claire La Berge points out, there is a long backstory to this, related to the transition from Keynesianism to neoliberalism and the corresponding shift from the tax-state to the debt-state.[25] While government spending on universities dropped dramatically, it didn't halt the circulation of cash within higher education ... it merely financialised it. Student loans are one obvious outcome, but universities have also turned to bond markets to fund their investments. Now university CEOs are able to present their institutions to wealthy corporations and individuals as a low-risk, tax-free investment.

Given the large sums involved, however, it isn't surprising that things can go wrong, as Reading University found out in 2019.[26] Under the leadership of Vice Chancellor Sir David Bell, a renowned educationalist, the university embarked on a risky joint venture in Malaysia. Its failure racked up millions in losses. To finance its operations, a £180 million debt was incurred with major banks. That's when Bell departed. The new acting Vice Chancellor later announced an investigation into why the university had been saddled with debts of £300 million. And as the vast new lecture halls are now in danger of remaining unused in post-Brexit and pandemic ravished England, this could literally signal the triumph of emptiness.

8.

One may debate the economic pros and cons of restructuring the university so that it runs like a large business firm. However, my argument is this: commercialisation has cultivated conditions in which it would be irrational *not* to despair. From an academic viewpoint at least, the transition has been incomprehensible. Encountering a diktat-issuing manager in Bank of America or BHP is something to be expected. Employees know what they're getting into. But in a university setting, it contradicts the values of collegiality and many of the reasons why we entered the profession in the first place. This growing disconnect has made higher education a dispiriting place to be. The recent spate of faculty (and student) suicides in the sector is but an extreme manifestation of this despondency. As Rosalind Gill remarks, offering compelling feminist insights on this issue, most academics find it hard to speak out and choose to suffer in silence instead, sometimes for years.[27]

The trouble is that this despair *is* actually difficult to voice, given the socio-political climate prevailing at the moment. No one wants HR knocking on the door or to even appear on their radar. Because the academic labour process has been so individualised open discontent tends to be framed as 'whinging' or 'biting the hand that feeds you'. Negativity is deemed a personal failing rather than a legitimate reaction to a needlessly callous environment. So we must analyse this despair from a structural perspective, as a consequence of the continuing commercialisation process.

Life in the Edu-Factory certainly hurts when we see academic values being swept aside by the juggernaut of economic rationalisation. But it's worse when colleagues and peers join in too. For example, while conversing with a mid-career academic at a conference some years back, I asked what she was working on. A paper for a leading journal I was told. 'Oh', I said, 'and what's it about?' She ignored the query and proceeded to reel off a number of other 'elite' journals she had submitted manuscripts to. After a while I gave up. It was disheartening. Whereas an idea was once worthy of consideration before any desire to publish, today the formula runs in the opposite direction. The measure has become the target and the tail is wagging the dog.

On the plane home from the conference I had a dark thought. I'd assumed that most academics felt a sense of *self-alienation* as they endured the verities of the neoliberal university. They think to themselves, 'although I'm trying to hit my annual targets, I realise this outward performance isn't the true reason I pursue an academic vocation'. But if current trends continue there's a good chance that in the future – one or two generations from now – academics will experience *no* internal contradiction whatsoever, having completely absorbed the new spirit of managerialism. Little will distinguish their jobs from those in a multinational enterprise or tyre factory. If that happens, then this book will be read as a curious relic from an alien and bygone age.

4

The Authoritarian
Turn in Universities

1.

The most dreadful experience I had with the authoritarian turn in higher education occurred when a new Head of Department was appointed. While sitting in my London office an email pinged and I opened it. Attached was a 'memo' from an administrator advising me of my teaching duties for the year and signed by our new boss. At a recent departmental meeting he'd told us that a few things were going to change around here. Zero faculty input regarding our teaching was a taste of things to come. The atmosphere grew miserable and I soon left for another university. A colleague who stayed later told me that access to the administration area was soon (electronically) barred to academics. Whereas once you dropped by to chat with a programme officer, a generic email address was now your only means of communication.

Open discussion about major issues facing departments and academics was once an integral part of how universities operated: not only out of choice, but *necessity* too given the highly trained, idiosyncratic and self-motivated workforce involved. This is different to what passes for 'consultation' today – a formal ritual designed to generate consent *after* crucial decisions have been made behind closed doors. As previously noted, universities have always had bureaucracy and authority. But corporatisation has radically reorganised how power, status and compliance intermix, both in a quantitative sense (the number of managers and administrators issuing orders) and qualitatively (the tone of authority exercised). On the surface, everything might look fine as a sort of faux consensus prevails. Technocrats devise procedures and academics respectfully follow them; 'an ecstasy of obedience' as British writer Marina Warner memorably described it after her brush with Essex University.[1] Dig a little deeper, however, and we uncover the dark underside of these top-down structures, especially in settings that otherwise require collegial cooperation and professional self-governance. Regular bureaucracy is shadowed by a troubling twin, what I term *darkocracy*. And as we'll see, the discontent it fuels (and sometimes feeds off) has converted universities into factories of sadness.

2.

A striking feature of the modern university has been the expansion of non-academic personnel vis-à-vis teaching and research faculty. The figures speak for themselves. Let's take the US: 450,000 faculty and 270,000 administrators were employed by universities in 1975.[2] By 2009 there were 728,977 full-time faculty (a 63 per cent increase) and 890,540 administrators (a 231 per cent increase). Another study found that universities hired around 520,000 non-academic administrators between 1987 and 2012 (or 87 every working day).[3] This incredible surge in both numbers and spending has outpaced student growth and appears to be correlated with the employment of casual teaching staff.[4] Similar patterns can be found in other countries. In the UK, academics are a minority (compared to managers, technicians, professionals and other non-teaching/non-research staff) in 71 per cent of the country's universities.[5] Academic staff numbers in Australia grew by 6773 between 2009 and 2016, whereas non-academic jobs grew by 10,327 and now outnumber academics 1.6 to 1.[6]

And then there's the growth of well-paid senior executives at the top of the organisational pyramid, occupying roles that seem to have materialised out of nowhere. As Benjamin Ginsberg amusingly notes in his book *The Fall of the Faculty*,

> Universities are filled with armies of functionaries – the vice presidents, associate vice presidents, assistant vice presidents, provosts, associate provosts, vice provosts, assistant provosts, deans, deanlets, deanlings, each commanding staffers and assistants – who, more and more, direct the operations of every school.[7]

None of this can be justified by increased student numbers, more complexity or the need for a wider division of labour in higher education. Nor can enhanced 'efficiency' (a cherished byword in the neoliberal lexicon) be behind it. The tsunami of bureaucratic sludge often makes completing even basic tasks a practical nightmare.[8] As anyone working in the tertiary sector will attest, disorganisation is the norm and the left hand doesn't know what the right hand is doing much of the time. Although it sounds counterintuitive, this reflects the universities attempt to emulate the corporate form, which celebrates executive chains of command, technical solutions above collegial deliberation and continuous programme/performance reviews. Governing academe in this manner is a recipe for serious trouble.

The problem is, according to Benjamin Ginsberg, with the exponential growth of managers and administrators, universities are soon driven by *their* imperatives, not the academics who teach and research. Deans and Provosts might still assert the importance of academic freedom, public education and intellectual curiosity. But only if such qualities are subservient to predetermined technocratic targets. Otherwise they're treated as an impediment to the smooth running of the enterprise.

To repeat, universities have always had administrators. Very important ones. Student-facing support staff, for example, perform an indispensable function. Payroll and the rest. Moreover, certain academic-led administrative roles – like Department Chair – are not new either and serve an important purpose. What we're concerned with instead, constituting the basis of 'darkocracy', are power networks controlled by functionaries in these institutions. Although some in their ranks may look like academics, many have been trained elsewhere or are career administrators. And those who were once scholars are now better labelled as *para-academics*, since they've acquired the 'boss syndrome' and find themselves looking down on their erstwhile colleagues with mild disdain.

By the same token, the impressive quantity of bureaucrats, administrators and managers isn't the main problem. It's something about their *character* that matters more. In short, university management today tends towards authoritarianism, sometimes overt, often hidden, but always experienced as pointlessly excessive by its recipients. These 'coercive bureaucracies' (as opposed to 'enabling' ones) have engendered a mood of dejection in higher education.[9] Academics obviously loathe command hierarchies given that their labour process relies upon the opposite: professional self-efficacy, collegial consensus and a degree of egalitarianism. The darkness evolves over time. It begins with outrage, transitions to frustration and finally settles as a deep-seated dismay. But seldom is it expressed as open rebellion (collective or otherwise). On those rare occasions when academics do resist, we gain a glimpse of the aggressive inner workings of darkocracy as it strikes back with malice, as I'll soon demonstrate.

3.

Top-down management structures are essentially about obedience and following orders, with little room for free community discussion or debate. At the end of the day, someone holds power over you no matter how cosy or friendly the relationship may seem. In this respect, university managerialism adheres to the essential tenets of Taylorism. Bosses are assumed to have superior information and insight compared to subordinates, which obviously doesn't go down too well in an academic setting. This managerial prerogative flows from the very top (the council, Vice-Chancellors, Presidents and Provosts) to the very bottom (teaching adjuncts, students). Hence why scrutiny always travels down the system, hardly ever up. We know nearly nothing about what happens above us (apart from generic email announcements), even though we probably ought to.

As a consequence, not only do academics frequently find the university apparatchik too autocratic, but also increasingly *superfluous* given how remote they seem from the value-adding activities on the ground. The 2020 Covid-19 pandemic really highlighted this administrative detachment. Senior managers don't teach, of course. So when presented with the formidable task of moving and delivering lessons online, they were mostly bystanders to the real action. In many institutions chaos reigned in the upper echelons. Some leaders retreated and disappeared. Whereas others became paranoid about the discretion afforded to frontline teaching staff and ramped up the surveillance.[10] But here's the ironic part. The goodwill, initiative and sheer amount of labour-time summoned by teaching faculty ensued not *because* of authority but *despite* it. Academics drew on many qualities – like their collective commitment to the vocation – that the corporate university has devalued for years.

When an intrinsically collegial institution is governed like a multinational enterprise (which is one of the *least* democratic places in our society, bar correctional facilities) then the chain of authority is sacrosanct. Don't be fooled by the argument that corporations in our post-modern age are flat and empowering tigers. Most remain sluggish and rigid behemoths that have cornered the market. I think this is why academic capitalism holds close ties with the rise of autocratic state capitalism and its cognate institutional forms. It's ironic. Under the aegis of market competition many universities (like most large corporations in the Western world) now bear an uncanny resemblance to organisations inspired by Xi Jinping.

Importantly, the contemporary university no longer *belongs* to academics, even if they continue to identify with it professionally and misinterpret the institution as a proxy for their vocation. To understand why, we must examine an ideological battle that's been raging in the background. Undoing this symbolic sense of collective 'ownership' was a major precondition for commercialising higher education, something that has spread throughout the public sphere. Subsequently, academics are no longer a collegium of peers but hired labour ... employees who sell their skill and availability to employers who enjoy true entitlement over the university. Consequently, academics are contractually obliged to do as they're told. It's unsurprising, then, that this mindset can open the door to more energetic expressions of authority, at least compared to earlier governance models.

If we add to this the urgency placed on *performance* (including KPIs and associated metrics, cocooned within a narrative of competition for students and/or governmental austerity) then the likelihood of friendly power structures emerging is pretty low. Bureaucracies are strange beasts at the best of times. They're especially notorious for multiplying their own ranks. Labour economist David Gordon noted this with respect to supervisors in US industry. Why were their numbers swelling? Gordon's answer is prescient: 'who keeps the supervisors honest? What guarantees that those supervisors won't be in cahoots with their charges? In such a hierarchy, you need supervisors to supervise supervisors ... and the supervisors above them ... and managers to watch the higher-level supervisors.'[11]

I think one reason why these hierarchies turned authoritarian in modern universities stems from the systemic application of neoclassical economic theory, including the principal/agency problem, moral hazard theory, contract theory, etc. These notions are built upon the assumption that economic agents should never be trusted. There's always a chance they'll shirk their duties and pursue an egotistical agenda. Hence the enormous importance placed on contracts and incentive systems today.[12] Applied to the employment relationship, each manager up and down the chain is encouraged to keep a watchful eye below them and expect the worst. A cold-hearted subjectivity invariably develops. Moreover, in this strictly 'results only' environment, functionaries are punished and/or rewarded according to outcomes. Over time senior administrators become institutionally numb to the feelings of those down the pecking order. Railroading through new policies and meeting deadlines assumes overarching importance, even if it means breaking a few eggs along the way. Unfortunately, some may even *enjoy* breaking those eggs. You never quite know how power and authority will affect people.

Many administrators are good people and also lament the managerialism that has mushroomed in universities.[13] Nevertheless, we must approach the question from a *structural* perspective, which is why identifying the specific qualities of darkocracy is crucial. For sure, as social psychologist Dacher Keltner discovered in a number of fascinating experiments, it makes no difference how 'nice' a person is, formal power automatically makes them less empathetic to those below them.[14] The reason why is simple. The power-holder isn't obliged to check their own behaviour as they would with equals.[15] This inbuilt psychological distance systematically increases one's sense of self-importance compared to those below. The influence can be so strong that powerful people sometimes believe that basic rules don't apply to them.[16] From here authoritarianism can easily sidle in.

We've all seen how this happens, even on a mundane level. Bosses above us (especially those we have regular contact with) might not have the courtesy to reply to an email or say thank you. For them you're not as important by default. However, one can be sure that she or he will suddenly display refined politeness when interacting with *their* superiors. Keltner's point is that the power hierarchy itself – minus the personalities involved – plays a vital part in turning ordinary people into inconsiderate oafs.

4.

Returning to David Gordon, he demonstrated how neoliberal corporations are not 'lean and mean' as business gurus extol, but 'fat and mean' instead. Perhaps the same path has been followed by the corporate university. Years of commercialisation and exposure to market forces hasn't transformed them into nimble business warriors, but over-bureaucratised Leviathans that treat dissent as a near treasonable offence.

Because productivity and outputs are narrowly defined as the only measure of success, more and more supervisors are hired to monitor academic staff and coax extra effort from them. This partially accounts for the chronic overwork that blights higher education today. It consists of what I call *real work* and *sludge work*. Real work are tasks that add genuine value to the institution in some shape or form, undertaken by both academics and support staff. For example, delivering a lecture or tutorial. Frontline student admissions' paperwork. IT support and maintenance. Academic oversight of a doctoral programme. Writing journal articles and books, etc. No doubt labour intensification has made 'real work' more demanding of late. But then we have 'sludge work' too. These are activities caused by over-bureaucratisation. Forms, procedures and mandatory exercises that add little intrinsic value, yet absorb significant amounts of time.

The problem with expansionist technocracies is that sooner or later all those managers have to justify their own positions. Generating pointless tasks or hoops for everyone to jump through is a classic way of doing this. It can transform the academic labour process into an overwhelming and exhausting experience. The Edu-Factory also changes how administrative staff behave. Their roles are no longer designed to minimise the burden of paperwork that academics undertake, but parcel it out to them via email. This is why faculty workloads are conspicuously *heavier* in universities that employ large numbers of administrators. Sludge work soon bleeds into real work, making it difficult to distinguish between the two. The biggest casualty is intellectual inquiry. Reading a book (let alone writing one) is considered an indulgence in this milieu, something best done in your own time. As a Dutch study recently concluded, 'if you love research, academia may not be for you … it may be easier to pursue your intellectual interests outside the university system'.[17]

But not all sludge work is created intentionally. Some is also an incidental off-shoot of the disgruntlement and lack of communication characteristic of big bureaucracies. Cleaning up other people's messes, usually entailing hours of emailing. Trying to fill the gaps caused by distant senior managers. Fighting fires (with students and colleagues) that are more symptomatic of their disempowerment than any substantive grievance. Duplication of tasks that could have been done once and so forth. This type of sludge work is soul-destroying because it *must* be undertaken if you want to get anything achieved but is formally unrecognised, since acknowledgement would signal a broader problem with the hierarchical order of things. Unlike hoop-jumping sludge work, this type of labour is necessary but essentially invisible, even when the emails turn hostile and tempers fray.

5.

This raises a significant point. My description of university bureaucracies might give the impression that they're highly formal, machine-like systems devoid of humanity. They are to an extent, of course. But something else is happening. Darkocracies also rely on an *informal* social dimension and that's when things get tricky.

Supervisors have a certain amount of discretion when it comes to managing staff and appraising their performance.[18] The scope of this discretion increases as one moves up the hierarchy. For subordinates, it means the everyday presentation of self becomes important. The personality trait universities desire most from academics are deference and tractability for sure, but with an added shot of loyalty.[19] This unspoken rule determines how favourably you are treated by management within the formal bureaucratic system. Patrimony is therefore pervasive in universities, mostly manifest behind closed doors. If a member of faculty fails to exhibit loyalty then they will suffer accordingly by being ignored, labelled a 'troublemaker' or given unappealing teaching duties. Dissenters are especially vulnerable to the unpredictable intrigues of darkocracy. Whereas most academics endeavour to quietly work around the bizarre forest of rules – keeping beneath the radar – open opposition is a different matter and is liable to attract retaliation.

US professor Ron Srigley gives a vivid example.[20] When the Vice President introduced a controversial new performance system it was met with little resistance since all 'were petrified of losing their positions'. One academic did speak up, however, sending an email to his small department outlining some concerns. Out of the blue, the troublemaker was called into the Vice President's office and told (in Srigley's words)

> he was naïve to think his university email account was not 'transparent' to his 'managers.' No discussion, no context, no actual accusation, and no reprimand. Just a thinly veiled threat that if he didn't watch out he'd find himself at the bottom of the academic East River ... He learned subsequently that his email account hadn't been compromised at all; he'd simply been betrayed by a fellow-traveling faculty member. Which means the president was just having a little fun threatening him.

Darkocracies thrive on these arbitrary and unaccountable expressions of power, including the backstabbing colleague who threw his fellow-traveller under the bus. What happened to Professor Thomas Docherty, renowned critic of the neoliberal university, offers an even more depressing example. In 2014 Warwick University accused him of 'inappropriate sighing' and directing 'negative vibes' at an ex-Head of Department. This earnt Docherty a nine-month suspension.[21]

In any organisational situation that individualises work, rebukes non-compliance and affords authority semi-discretionary powers when managing others, bullying is almost inevitable. It is said to be rife in the UK higher education sector, with senior administrators, 'star' professors and other influential officials the main culprits.[22] An Australian study found one quarter of 22,000 staff from 19 institutions had been victims of harassment and bullying. Among women, it was one in three. So why do victims rarely report it? Because that isn't how darkocracies work unfortunately. A university's complaints system is often overseen by the very authority structure in question.[23] As political scientist David West observes:

... complaint procedures take place within the organizational hierarchy that produced the complaint in the first place, a hierarchy designed to confer authority on superiors and induce obedience in subordinates. Senior managers are, by the institutional logic of their position, inclined to support immediate subordinates who are the objects of a complaint. Finding in favour of the manager has the advantage of reinforcing the message that managerial instructions should be obeyed.[24]

What about the Human Resource department? Aren't they meant to protect employees from this type of harassment? In theory, yes. But HR *always* defers to senior management, who in turn seek to minimise the adverse publicity a grievance might attract. They may also be the bullying aggressor themselves.[25] In other words, when a boss is involved, victims of bullying simply cannot trust HR and so often keep quiet and try to work around the problem instead.

6.

On a more general level, HR features prominently in darkocracies since they act as enforcers or, as some might say, 'hitmen', for senior executives, especially during industrial disputes. While managers see them as friendly support, employees tend to view HR as a threatening entity whom they would rather avoid if possible.[26] This represents a historical shift from the rather benign role of personnel management (dealing with payroll, etc.) to a more legal-supervisory function, propelled by the wider contractualisation of society. While presenting a pleasant professional development gloss to their job, including work-life balance programmes and 'Fun Fridays', HR usually performs the dirty work for deans and deanlets. Their loyalty to management is undying. They would happily *fire themselves* if the nomenclature ordered it. A HR consultant recently confessed, as a department, it is purely there to support senior management. I have seen cases where HR staff, deemed to be too employee-focused, are actually got rid of. I've been in HR for most of my career and while we were very much there to help initially, that has evolved to the other extreme.[27]

What she really means by 'evolution' is the neoliberalisation of employment relations, which stresses power differentials between management and staff, labour and capital, rich and poor and so on. HR's role is to manage the instabilities caused by market individualism and keep a lid on any potential unrest that may ensue. For instance, during the UK 2018 pensions dispute, HR sent all sorts of threatening emails to teaching staff, suggesting they'd be held personally liable if students sued the university for refunds. It was a classic standover tactic designed to instil fear and doubt. So much for 'Fun Fridays'.

The pensions strike and similar high-prolife clashes are obviously undesirable to the neoliberal university. The governors of darkocracy would prefer to dispense with conflict on a discrete and individual basis. In order to minimise negative publicity, therefore, Non-Disclosure Agreements (NDAs) or 'gagging orders' are now in vogue. They were originally designed to protect firms from losing valuable trade secrets when employees departed the organisation. Universities now love NDAs, deploying them to move individuals out of the institution with minimal reputational damage, including whistle-blowers and victims of sexual harassment and/or bullying: signees are prohibited from publicly disparaging their former employer or discussing the incident in question. Instead of suing, rallying union support or going to the media, the situation is quietly defused with a NDA and lump sum cash payment. Between 2017 and 2019 UK universities spent £87 million on gagging orders, entailing 4000 settlements.[28] It's an easy way out for universities, with minimal inconvenience … for them, at least. As one sexual harassment victim observed, 'universities would rather pay off people to leave, than push out the person doing the bullying'.[29] Indeed, perhaps it's only a matter of time before NDAs are used to prohibit critical investigations of the neoliberal university itself.

7.

Most studies endeavouring to link disorders of the soul (depression, anxiety, paranoia, suicide ideation, etc.) with neoliberal capitalism focus on market individualism. Not only does it isolate people from each other but makes them solely responsible for what are in fact socio-economic forces. In the words of Mark Fisher, feeling like a 'good for nothing' is instilled among the vast losers of this cut-throat game from the outset.[30] But I think we must also examine the harms wrought by neoliberalism's bureaucratic collectivism; psychic pathologies that flow not from the lack of people, but a surfeit of the wrong kind, microsocial pressures that get under your skin. This isn't simply about failed economic subjects being blamed for their misfortunes. A university worker might be relatively secure, but that's no protection from the ills inflicted on a different register by dark bureaucracies. These maladies are secretly carried around with us and repressed until finally vented, usually at home or in our dreams.

Let's conduct a small thought experiment. Imagine a young academic who is otherwise confident (but not overly so), comfortable with themselves (yet seeking to advance their career), displays a sunny disposition (with a healthy dose of intellectual scepticism) and is passionate about their chosen discipline. They understand the importance of collegiality because it helped them through their graduate studies. They now look forward to embarking on a long and fulfilling career.

What emotional challenges would this otherwise sane and stable person encounter upon entering the corporate university today?

To begin with, the power hierarchies we've examined are not only objective but psychological too. They impute bosses with a sense of superiority. And by turns the subordinate always feels inferior and less worthy comparatively speaking. When accentuated in a social system, the impression of *insignificance* can grow and erode one's self-confidence. This elicits a number of responses, many of which are not healthy. Individuals may overcompensate by becoming egoistical careerists, continually reminding anyone within earshot of how great they are. Others might simply try harder, not realising that contemporary appraisals systems are designed to ensure *everyone* falls short in some shape or form. This introduces *anxiety* into the mix, which today is an ordinary part of university life.

Our imaginary academic would then experience the stress associated with relentless measurement and evaluation. Are you good enough? Do you have what it takes to be an excellent researcher? For those facing the daunting North American tenure-track system, these metrics make or break careers and the pressure to perform is intense. Schools may confer 'star' status on certain academics, praising them with awards and acolytes. This stokes a sense of inadequacy and/or competition among everyone else. Most neoliberal university performance reviews, however, are based on the principle of continuous improvement, so an element of *self-doubt* touches even the most accomplished scholar. Add gender and race inequalities into the formula (universities remain dominated by white males), then these feelings of worthlessness are often amplified.[31]

Any academic entering this cultural system will also have to navigate social power at the informal level. Have I been amenable enough to my Departmental Chair? They didn't reply to my email invitation regarding an upcoming talk, is something wrong? Did I mess up somehow? Has a jealous colleague spread lies about me? Darkocracies are highly *neurotic* environments, mainly played out offstage in one's private life. Repeating a hypothetical encounter with a co-worker or supervisor in your head over and over again, for example. This soon begins to affect personal relationships too.

Our young scholar will inevitably meet some very unhappy colleagues. These disgruntled individuals seldom direct their vitriol at its source – a supervisor, promotions committee or dean – for obvious reasons. So they displace it sideways, towards more accessible targets (colleagues, junior administrators, students, etc.). Professional envy and sabotage may also feature here. And invariably a psychopath or two will be quietly prowling the hallways. As our imaginary academic goes about their daily business, he or she will naturally avoid these unpleasant co-workers. Over time, the thought of coming into the office may fill them with dread. Thank god for email they half-joke. It's hell ... but a lesser one. Coronavirus has a silver lining after all.

And finally, given the high levels of 'real work' and 'sludge work' our young scholar will conduct over a prolonged period, they'll soon display symptoms of extreme fatigue: these include chronic tiredness, insomnia, irritability, aching muscles, impaired judgement and alcohol abuse.

Feeling inadequate and stressed. Neurotic and paranoid. Dreading the office. Highly irritable and unhappy. Constantly tired and addicted to office email. Our imaginary academic is now a creature of the neoliberal university. The labour of love they once knew has somehow opened a black hole at the centre of their being. Before long, the darkness closes in.

5

You're Not a Spreadsheet With Hair

1.

I was recently chatting with a lecturer about the university's preoccupation with numerical measurements or 'metrics' and she mentioned her institution was introducing *dashboards*. Piquing my curiosity, I asked what she meant. Her dashboard is a digitalised interface that used 'big data' techniques to collate information about academic research publications (including their quality as defined by journal ranking lists and impact scores), grant applications, individual citations and so forth. The data is presented on a single screen in easily readable bar graphs and Venn diagrams. While it was meant to help scholars plan their careers, supervisors and senior management could also access the information for appraisal purposes.

My friend explained that her dashboard was a 'real time' platform and updated in a continuous fashion. Was the data accurate, I asked? 'No, of course not' she smiled. As far as my dashboard is concerned she said, 'I barely have a pulse.' I had to laugh. The moment big data meets suboptimal bureaucracy, it's never going to end well.

When pop singer Lorde protested, 'I'm not a spreadsheet with hair!' she was lamenting how the music industry had reduced her existence to a walking sales figure. And a fairly lucrative one at that. Lorde's lament, however, would fall on deaf ears in the corporate university, where an impressive range of digital metrics, ranking systems and big data platforms are all the rage.

Production stats and performance figures are nothing new, of course. But in higher education today, a veritable 'tyranny of metrics', to borrow Jerry Muller's phrase, tracks almost everything we do.[1] Student satisfaction scores, sometimes surveyed two or three times per semester; journal quality rankings like Scimago and ISI, in addition to discipline-level tables that typically carry a 1–4 (including 4*) or A–D scale to convey prestige; impact factors for leading journals; research grant application submissions and successful external income; Google citation ratings and the notorious H-Index designed to capture both productivity (or quantity) and impact (or quality). This barrage of data is then recalibrated to university-specific templates and used during annual appraisals, helping to allocate workloads (including teaching relief for 'star' academics, etc.), assess promotion and tenure eligibility or guide the much-feared 'Performance Improvement Plan' for staff who won't knuckle under.

The story doesn't end there, however. For those who enter upper-management, yet another wall of numbers appears, punctuated by KPIs, Gantt Charts and budgetary targets. As for the cherry on top, let's not forget that universities as a whole are placed on national (and global) league tables like QS World University Rankings, U.S. News and World Report's Best Colleges and Times Higher Education World University Rankings, supposedly signalling their quality vis-à-vis competitors, much like the controversial Research Excellence Framework (or REF) in the UK. In the US, this culminated with the 2013 launch of Obama's 'College Scorecard' system. It gathers massive amounts of data about universities so students can make informed investment decisions.

2.

This obsession with metrics and big data originates from a number of sources. Clearly there's an attempt to mimic private enterprises that have always closely measured productivity, outputs and earnings. In the UK, for example, this gained traction with the 1985 Jarratt Report which recommended universities be managed with strict accounting controls, budgetary constraints and performance targets.[2] Academic consensus and collegiality were especially flagged for substantial reform since big corporations didn't work that way. Most academic committees – where issues are discussed and collectively decided upon – were a waste of time according to ex-businessman Sir Alex Jarratt. Executive authority was far more efficient. And metrics could capture those efficiencies with methodical precision.

Today the function of management accounting – which price controls an organisation's internal operations – is being digitalised as big data becomes fashionable. Public sector institutions find an additional justification for this metric-fetish: taxpayers demanding transparency, accountability and value for money. However, reducing transparency to an abstract set of numbers is notoriously misleading. Figures can distort the truth as much as unveil it. Nevertheless, a tireless 'audit culture' has blossomed in universities around the world, with spreadsheet-reliant bosses and IT-nerds leading the way.[3]

Yet another excuse for this quant-attack is *merit*. Good researchers and teachers, for example, ought to be rewarded fairly, whereas in the past an 'old boy network' was commonplace. In that previous system, academics might be objectively poor performers but socially well connected and end up receiving all the glory, while those displaying genuine teaching/publishing excellence are ignored. There's a modicum of truth to this. However, the narrative typically omits the more unsavoury part of the solution. What's meant to be a neutral indicator of one's worth may dislodge the old boys' club. But it doesn't dissolve social domination by any means. In this respect, transparency entails a dark side that is paradoxically obscured by all this data.

Numbers provide administrators with an easy method for monitoring and regulating work. So far so good. But this component of 'metrification' was perceptively called into question by Chris Lorenz when he asked: if you're so smart, then why are you under so much surveillance?[4] It's a great question. Academics are often pictured – including by themselves – as semi-autonomous professionals who largely manage their own activities for the greater good of the institution. But recall how the corporate university has reconfigured the employment relationship in accordance with neoclassical economics. Collegial self-governance (where each member behaves as collective custodians of the enterprise) has been replaced by an insider/outsider dyad: namely employers and employees. The interests of academics, it's assumed, are not necessarily aligned with employers and so micromanagement is warranted. This assumption usually comes to light during periods of upheaval, such as the pensions dispute in the UK or the post-Covid-19 crackdown. Most importantly, the medium of metrics contains an important message: numbers on a spreadsheet aren't supposed to talk back.

The ideology of merit is also closely linked to market rationality. Academics are encouraged to act like independent business owners, constantly polishing their CVs and leveraging their position for better income. Having a quantified representation of one's market value fits into this vision of academic capitalism hand in glove. The concept has been taken to extremes, with the REF perhaps epitomising the unintended consequences as academics jostle in the UK labour market, jumping from one institution to another. In that case, economic individualism clearly interlinks with the institutional drive to track and measure everything scholars do in higher education.

3.

Why does administrative technocracy almost inevitably attract the excessive quantification of academic labour we see in universities today? The answer lies in the collapse of *quality* into *quantity*, which is a prime symptom of managerialism. Numbers are easier to collect and give senior decision-makers a seductive illusion of control. The assumption is that figures don't lie (unlike real people), something David Beer terms a 'data imaginary', an attitude that can become so abstract and remote that administrators lose touch with reality.[5] So it simply wasn't the case that before this transformation no one knew what was going on in universities. Managers, academics and administrators did, of course. But their knowledge was anchored to a set of more qualitative governance ideals, which is very different today.

This touches upon an important issue. The digitalised and overmeasured university is primarily inspired by control rather than functional coordination. Hence why these institutions bear little resemblance to those lean, flexible and market-supple enterprises so often lionised in neoclassical theory. There's no such thing as an entrepreneurial university. It's more common to find autocratic and centralised structures that rely on quantification to surveil and prod its workforce. Signs of this heavy-handed quantification are everywhere. Faculty at the UC Berkeley, for example, were shocked to discover their internet activity was being closely scrutinised by electronic-spyware and the data regularly reviewed by management.[6] An alarmed professor said this included 'all email, all the websites you visit, all the data you receive from off campus or data you send off campus'. At other universities staff attendance is digitally recorded and used for HR purposes at a later date. After all, as with other major industrial complexes, the Edu-Factory doesn't tolerate absenteeism or shirking, so punch-in like everyone else, an injunction rendered even more invasive and complex during the 2020 Coronavirus debacle.

No wonder some have compared contemporary university administration to the USSR under Joseph Stalin.[7] When linked to performance outputs (and the punitive repercussions awaiting those who fail to achieve), the Soviets perfected a 'targets and terror' system, as illustrated by the infamous Stakhanovite movement.[8] But their methods were less daunting in one important respect. The Soviets measured and ranked *teams*. Whereas the corporate university spotlights *individuals* instead, which (from management's perspective at least) helps induce the atomised exposure demanded by neoclassical economics. It's this individualising tendency blended with the blind abstractions of quantification that allows the Edu-Factory to hone its own unique brand of 'terror'.

Does this cornucopia of numbers tell us what's objectively happening in university divisions and departments? Only partly. And do they really motivate faculty to become better academics? Probably not. Let's take a rather pedestrian example commonly seen today. When a list of the 'top ten lecturers' is circulated by senior administrators, student satisfaction scores are presumably the metric used. An email like this is intended to confer recognition on those teaching well and encourage the rest who didn't make the list. If financial rewards are included, then the announcement obviously attracts added attention. However, much is missed in this simple ranking exercise. No lecturer is an island. There's a good chance other colleagues and administrative staff were working behind the scenes and assisting 'star' teachers to deliver great classes.

Performance metrics overlook this unmeasurable background activity – including cooperation, goodwill and collegiality – and artificially sequester staff from their organisational surroundings. The numbers only tell a manager that John has produced 80 widgets this week and Samantha 30. That Samantha may have helped John when he was in a bind doesn't compute. Thus there's a good chance that the 'top ten lecturers' email will demotivate those who helped but weren't recognised. And subsequently, they might think twice about being so generous next time.

Metric-mania prompts other dysfunctions that are endemic in the neoliberal university. For instance, performance measurement platforms (like the digital dashboard described earlier) favour *immediacy*, and present a relatively short-term picture of academic effort. This is then included in annual performance reviews or even shorter cycles in high-performance institutions. But given the complex and time-intensive labour process that defines genuine scholarly work – say, publishing in a top-tier journal or writing a well-regarded book – this short-termism can be very misleading. Using a rather American-centric example to make the point, Jerry Muller discusses the mission to capture Osama Bin Laden: 'the intelligence analysts who ultimately located Osama Bin Laden worked on the problem for years. If measured at any point, the productivity of those analysts would have been zero. Month after month, their failure rate was 100 per cent, until they achieved success.'[9]

Consequently, metrics often contain a temporal bias, triggering a desire to display rapid results by those being measured. The institutional acceleration that ensues can seriously confound the endogenous rhythms of academic work.[10] I've seen it more than once. A scholar who apparently produces nothing for two years is harassed by the university until they finally look for a job elsewhere, to only then publish the field-changing paper they'd been working on all that time. Managers under the spell of metric short-termism find it impossible to attune their mental schemas to the *longue durée* of deep scholarship. They instead prioritise a deceptive mode of immediacy, reflecting no doubt their own KPIs and reward structures.

4.

These dynamics explain the raft of *unintended consequences* that the overuse of metrics precipitates. For example, the short-termism mentioned above can actually dissuade academics from investing years in their respective field, including the prolonged exertion needed to write a prestigious paper. A system designed to measure and reward 'excellence' ends up discouraging the very behaviour necessary for excellence. Let's return to digital dashboarding. The culture of peer comparison it fosters may undermine collaboration and camaraderie in a school, especially if individual dashboards are accessible to colleagues. Or take that email celebrating the 'top ten lecturers' mentioned earlier. There's a good chance it will leave everyone else in the department dejected, even the teacher who came a close 11th and received no praise. This might sound trifling, but over time it creates a feedback loop. Staff omitted from the 'top ten lecturers' list may simply give up, including that unrecognised 11th best teacher. Nor can our 'star performers' insulate themselves from the wider resentment that ensues. The more conscientious begin to feel guilty. Why weren't the colleagues who helped me acknowledged too? All of this is made worse when the email is sent by a senior manager who hasn't delivered an undergraduate lecture in years … or ever.

In the hyper-competitive atmosphere of the neoliberal university, the negative self-evaluations that metrics encourage eventually takes a toll on trust, cooperation and overall job satisfaction.

Depressing examples of this come from the private sector, firms like Amazon, which universities adore as entrepreneurial path-finders. A *New York Times* investigation of professional workers at Amazon presents a textbook case of unintended consequences.[11] We already knew how bad conditions were in Amazon's ware-houses, but no one expected their well-paid white-collar staff or 'Amazonians' had become traumatised wrecks as well. Long hours was only the start. The company teased that its standards were 'unreasonably high'. If a manager sent an email after midnight, sleeping employees would soon receive a text message asking why they hadn't replied.

But it was Jeff Bezos' data-obsessed management style that caused the most misery. Nearly every facet of office life was quan-tified and monitored. Amazonians were encouraged to use an anonymous feedback system (Anytime Feedback Tool), relaying information to superiors about their co-workers: 'I felt concerned about his inflexibility and openly complaining about minor tasks.' This feedback was duly converted into numerics and fed into the machine for later evaluation. None of this would matter much if it wasn't for Amazon's infamous rank-and-yank policy. Having collected and processed the data, employees were periodically stack-ranked, with those at the bottom automatically eliminated. Soon the anonymous feedback system was used to sabotage rivals and a climate of paranoia prevailed. Employees wept at their desks and work overshadowed everything: 'it's as if you've got the C.E.O. of the company in bed with you at 3 a.m. breathing down your neck', one weary office worker remarked.

As it falls in love with big data, the idea of this management system being replicated in universities doesn't bear thinking about. But I'm sure it is being considered. The rank-and-yank perfor-mance appraisal is an excellent example – *in extremis* – of how metrics can screw up an organisation. Quotas in this context (like firing the bottom 10 per cent of employees no matter what) rely on a false distribution curve. For example, imagine (using conventional quality metrics) a university somehow hires the world's top ten macromolecular biochemists. They represent the crème de le crème, a fraction of the academics active in the field. Now let's stack-rank these ten individuals, with the bottom 10 per cent told they're useless and threatened with termination. From this perspective, the biochemist who comes 10th is clearly inferior to his or her colleague in 1st place – 90 per cent so in fact. But in the wider scheme of things, the differences between them are not worth mentioning. Both are brilliant. Up to a point, the same weakness plagues *all* ranking systems in highly trained and diverse professional communities, which is made worse if the measurement method contains biases favouring male academics, for example, as opposed to female or non-Western ones, etc.

Given all this social quantification, one might expect the 'human side' of academia to be all but expunged from university campuses, turning faculty into unfeeling robots. But the exact opposite occurs; some human-all-too-human emotions invariably simmer beneath the surface, including distress, anxiety and secret fears of being fired. Neuroticism and numbers are not distant cousins. Moreover, management easily can take on a *more* judgemental flavour when staff are overseen in this way. After all, those detailed spreadsheets demand interpretation, otherwise they're a waste of time. This is when metrics intersect with departmental politics and quants become a proxy for your social standing, frequently wrapped in the language of moralism. Recent studies have revealed as much: the more universities adopt tough performance metrics, the more subjective and arbitrary those work environments tend to feel.[12]

It's not just individual-to-individual comparisons that can dismantle occupational wellbeing and productivity. In the dog-eat-dog world of higher education, entire schools and universities can succumb to the craze, something Wendy Espeland and Michael Sauder demonstrate in US law schools.[13] As they observed, 'nearly everyone we spoke to lived in dread of the inevitable day that new rankings had come out showing their school had dropped to a worse number or tier, and many of the changes caused by the rankings can be directly traced to this fear'.[14]

What changes are Espeland and Sauder referring to? Modified behaviour caused by ranking cycles reached into the very grain of institutions, including career services, classroom practices, academics publishing and daily administration. Increased bureaucracy was activated to measure and reward performance. Deans relentlessly reminded schools they weren't yet good enough and needed to up their game. Hypostatised numbers, often semi-detached from actual activity on the ground, were worshiped as imperial truths by decision-makers, who consequently saw deficiencies everywhere they looked. Even schools at the very top of the league tables, who ought to be basking in the glory, were overwhelmed with anxiety, terrified of losing that leading spot. According to Espeland and Sauder, this metric-fixation is the main reason why law schools have become such horrid places to work.

5.

University performance metrics are designed not only to measure behaviour but incentivise it in certain directions. Under such circumstances, it's inevitable that some try to game the system. This raises the thorny problem of *perverse incentives* that can render performance metrics not only useless, but downright dangerous. They appear anytime a measure becomes the target, sometimes called 'Goodhart's Law'. An oft-quoted example is nineteenth century French colonists trying to eradicate rat infestation in Hanoi. Authorities offered locals a financial bounty for every rat tail handed in.[15] The result was mass rat farming on the outskirts of town and an impressive increase in the rodent population.

With its reliance on economic quantification, neoliberal capitalism specialises in this dysfunction. For example, incentivised sales teams in the financial services industry led banks to sell products to customers who didn't really need them. Wells Fargo even opened fake accounts to meet their targets.[16] Shareholder capitalism encourages CEOs to increase the share price no matter what, even if it means harming the firm in the process. Hence Jack Walsh's famous quip that shareholder value 'is the dumbest idea in the world. Shareholder value is a result, not a strategy …'.

When the measure becomes the target, perverse incentives undermine academic work in pretty much the same way. The most obvious example can be found in lecture halls. Now that teachers are evaluated by students on a five-point Likert scale, and those results are factored into promotion and tenure decisions, all sorts of weird things begin to happen. What makes a student 'satisfied' isn't always conducive to sound pedagogy. Hence two major challenges that dog corporatised universities today: grade inflation and teaching content that some might mistake for entertainment. As one astute commentator recently remarked, this is really about the inner contradictions of commoditised education: 'standards decline, so students learn less as the cost of their education rises. Ironically, this happens because students are now considered customers, so colleges want to keep them happy.'[17]

Gaming academia – where the measurement method is manipulated to one's benefit – takes several forms. Mark Edwards and Siddhartha Roy present a comprehensive overview of the tactics used.[18] The main driver of perverse incentives, they suggest, is not metrics per se, but broader forces linked to government funding cuts, scarce resource allocation and the university's deification of 'excellence' above all. Once the 'publish or perish' panic consumes a workforce, anything can happen – 70 per cent of university researchers suspect their peers are manipulating the system in this respect, gaining an unfair advantage while still playing by the rules.[19] A predictable self-rationalisation then follows: if everyone else is doing it, then why not me? Edwards and Roy reflect on this when discussing the meritocracy arguments universities have used to embed this audit culture: 'ultimately, the well-intentioned use of quantitative metrics may create inequities and outcomes worse than the systems they replaced. Specifically, if rewards are disproportionally given to individuals manipulating their metrics, problems of the old subjective paradigms (e.g., old boy networks) may be tame by comparison.'[20]

Let's focus on research. Here are some perverse incentives that many academics will recognise:

Incentive: Reward researchers for increased publications.
Intended effect: Improve research productivity and performance.
Actual outcome: Growth in substandard papers, incremental-orientated research, increase in false or misleading use of data.

Incentive: Reward researchers for increased citations.
Intended effect: Reward influential and impactful research.
Actual outcome: Lengthy and instrumental self-referencing, journal reviewers and editors insisting their own papers be cited.

Incentive: Reward authors who publish papers in top-ranking journals.
Intended effect: Encourage research excellence.
Actual outcome: Authors have little interest in the actual 'content' of their articles, diminishing innovation in the field, bestowing elite journals with tremendous powers.[21]

Journal article publishing is a major part of this institutionalised anxiety and the gaming that follows. Careers hang in the balance and journals hold the key because they dominate academic reward systems, including tenure and promotion. This makes them especially susceptible to perverse incentives, not to mention backroom deals and wrangling. Is it a coincidence that most so-called top journals are based at the wealthiest universities, particularly in the US? But it gets murkier. I've heard that some institutions are happy to fund workshops in desirable locations, flying in senior editors to comment on papers, which are later submitted to their journals. I'm not saying the game is entirely rigged, but it's not a level playing field by any stretch.

A big winner in all this are the corporations that own many major academic journals. Their dubious business model is now infamous, with multinational firms effectively extorting universities with outlandish subscription fees, despite the fact that universities ultimately pay for the labour that produces the content. Springer, Wiley and Emerald among others consequently enjoy incredible profit margins, so much so that one commentator exclaimed that, academic publishers make Murdoch look like a socialist.[22]

6.

The pressure to publish is now immense. Even established professors are getting flustered. This underlies the most serious perverse incentive in academia to date: the temptation to misrepresent/falsify data in order to get published in prestigious outlets.

P-hacking (named after the 'p-value' that detects statistical significance), for example, has received much attention in disciplines using statistical modelling and quantitative methodologies. The trouble begins when journals in psychology, marketing and medicine, just to name a few, are more interested in confirmatory findings than null-hypotheses (that reveal no significant correlation).[23] Because jobs, salaries and promotions are closely tied to publishing in these influential outlets, some Primary Investigators are willing to massage the data a bit to get more attractive results. Also known as data-dredging, p-hacking involves running statistical analyses many times over until a confirmatory pattern (a positive <.05 statistical finding) emerges randomly. This will happen perhaps 1 per cent of the time, and certainly isn't representative of the data as a whole. For example, a drug designed to halt Alzheimer's might yield a null-hypothesis in 99.5 per cent of trials. However, there's a 0.5 per cent chance of $p < .05$ significance, caused by random extraneous factors, etc. *That* result is then published. Related tricks like HARKing (where confirmatory hypotheses are added only *after* a statistical significance is found) and 'dry-labbing' (where the experiment lab exists only on paper) risk completely derailing the legitimacy of quantitative research.

In order to find Eldorado and see their name in that elusive world leading journal, some academics sadly go even further. The recent rise in research fraud obviously stems from the 'publish or perish' ethos encouraged in the Edu-Factory. Indeed, it's testimony to the enduring integrity of academic scholarship that, despite the pressure to do so, *more* aren't up to no good. Misreporting findings or simply fabricating data has led to a number of embarrassing scandals in the academy. Journal article retraction rates have skyrocketed as a result. The case of Tilburg University social psychologist, Professor Diederik Stapel stands out. Over the course of several decades Professor Stapel published papers containing bogus data. When he gave the figures to his doctoral students to tabulate, they were shocked to find that different experiments had miraculously created the exact same results – a near impossibility, of course. It turned out that Stapel had got tired of faking massive datasets each time and recycled the same spreadsheet for different papers. After the fraud was discovered, 58 articles were retracted, including one in *Science*.

It is easy to understand why the academic community crucified Diederik Stapel for his devious behaviour. However, a government investigation also apportioned blame to his peer group. First, Stapel was partially a product of a cut-throat competitive environment, revealing an occupational-wide malaise that cannot be explained away by a few bad apples. Second, Stapel had become a powerful figure in his discipline. The authority he wielded generated unhealthy levels of deference and compliance among fellow scholars. As the panel remarked,

> It is almost inconceivable that co-authors who analysed the data intensively, or reviewers of the international 'leading journals', who are deemed to be experts in their field, could have failed to see that a reported experiment would have been almost infeasible in practice, did not notice the reporting of impossible statistical results.[24]

To repeat, no academic is an island, including both its 'stars' and pariahs.

7.

So where does that leave us with respect to the use of metrics in higher education? Should we return to the pre-dashboarding days, when academic quality and productivity was determined through experienced judgement? I've seen a number of universities and schools try and reverse (or at least moderate) the over-quantification of scholarship and teaching. It was more difficult than they thought. For one thing, the whole governmental funding structure has cemented these metrics into academia, making it the primary language we speak. This has totally colonised how senior managers think in universities. Most institutions would find it unimaginable to convene a tenure committee, for example, without screeds of data to help them decide.

Furthermore, many academics have invested their careers in journal rankings, league tables and related scoring systems. The sunk costs are significant. Thus even those who are critical of performance metrics might still rejoice when they see their Google Citation Score increase. Lecturers may be fully aware that student satisfaction surveys aren't a great gauge of pedagogical quality but strive to get good scores nevertheless since management take them seriously. In other words, there's a chance that doing things differently would be resisted by faculty not because they *like* metrics but because their careers have become so reliant on them. All the same, everything about us that isn't quantifiable is now desperately searching for a way out.

6

The Demise of *Homo Academicus*

1.

September 2019.

19-year-old University of Canterbury (New Zealand) student Mason Pendrous was found dead in his campus dormitory room.[1] The tragedy attracted media attention due to the unusual circumstances surrounding his death. Fellow students in the halls of residence detected a foul smell coming from his room located at the end of a dark hallway. Police were alerted and forced entry into the tiny bedroom, making the gruesome discovery. Judging by the state of decomposition, the corpse had lain undisturbed for a month.[2] Mason Pendrous' death was not treated as suspicious by police. Nor did they find any signs of illicit drug use. The inevitable question was raised: how could a student die and go unnoticed for weeks in a busy, highly social environment like this?

University officials quickly went into damage control mode, reassuring everyone that 'comprehensive pastoral care programmes' are an essential part of on-campus accommodation. It turned out that the dormitory wasn't actually managed by the university but Australian firm Campus Living Villages. It accommodates 45,000 students worldwide in similar facilities. A senior spokesman was asked why the death went undetected for so long. This housing is designed to provide 'maximum independence', he replied.[3] Privacy is paramount. For example, cleaners only service communal areas regularly and not rooms. Dining is left to the student's discretion. Many found the argument flimsy, however, with the Minister of Education summing up the prevailing mood: 'no student should be left for that period of time unattended, uncared for, when they're living in a hall of residence or a hostel'.[4]

Pendrous' death was shocking not just because it symbolised the lonely individualism of a society besieged by economic rationalism. To die and go unnoticed is something we occasionally hear happening to elderly folk in some forgotten wasteland on the outskirts of Leicester ... but not in a thriving university hall of residence teeming with young people. Something had gone very wrong here. Clearly this was no ordinary 'student village' ...

2.

The days when students led relatively carefree and bohemian lives are definitely over, no matter how often neocons chide millennial 'snowflakes' for their safe spaces and trigger warnings.[5] Within the span of a few decades, student culture has become isolating, high-pressured and anxious, reflecting the norms of late capitalism as a whole. Universities are no longer sanctuaries from market discipline, but one of its central expressions. Following Mason Pendrous' death, a crowd-funding campaign was launched to raise money for his loved ones. Only it turned out to be a scam. An unscrupulous individual was attempting to cash-in on the public sympathy.[6] Welcome to New Zealand, a country that has been privatised to death.

This morbid story raises three important points concerning the dark undercurrents changing the face of higher education today. The first pertains to the commercial logic of Pendrous' housing situation, where impersonal market forces replace conventional accommodation arrangements. Would the 19-year-old's body have been discovered earlier if his 'student village' was managed by the university rather than a distant multinational subcontractor? Or by students themselves? Perhaps. The plush sociality we'd expect in an expensive dorm like this had been recrafted for 'maximum independence', a phrase that has weird penal undertones. We can still find forms of sociality even in the most commercialised situations, of course, since markets require exchange and reciprocity. But it's shot through by the depersonalising distance of money and instrumental reason. When cash is universalised in this manner life too assumes a rather abstract hue, even in the shoulder-to-shoulder bustle of the *agora*. Once the transaction is done, for better or worse you're on your own. Proper villages don't function like this for obvious reasons.

Mason Pendrous' death also highlights the perverse intersection of personal freedom and social abandonment, a salient effect of neoclassical economics when applied to actual social settings. What 19-year-old wouldn't want to be left alone, free from the constraints of mum and dad? And no doubt Campus Living Villages found the idea attractive too. Playing a surrogate parent is expensive. Ensuring 'maximum independence' is a neat way to reduce operating costs. Fewer cleaners and cooks. But here's the catch. Following years of marketisation we've learned that true individual freedom cannot be realised via the medium of societal abandonment. It requires a vibrant and robust social backdrop. This is why Pendrous found personal desolation instead of liberation within this microcosm of hyper-independence. What more epitomises the cultural antinomies of free market capitalism than dying alone and unnoticed in a crowded housing complex?

The second issue concerns why Mason Pendrous' fellow students didn't notice his absence until weeks after his death. Even if shy and solitary, it still seems inconceivable that his local community could be so wafer-thin. Having said that, while being processed in the Edu-Factory, students are put under immense pressure to complete their degrees, often while holding down part-time jobs and servicing debt obligations. This inevitably isolates people and normalises the ritual of overwork. Idle socialising may seem like a waste of time, an indulgence. As one Australian student recently remarked, 'university is sold as an enjoyable, socially prosperous time in the lives of young adults. But for some, it's a time of confronting and disappointing realisations about university life. Loneliness is difficult to quantify but not hard to spot.'[7] Market individualism – *principium individuationis* – erodes community bonds not because it makes people selfish and greedy, but because they're often too busy to meaningfully interact with each other, leaving them to deal with the mounting stress alone.

And third, the institutional logic of the university itself must be questioned. Weren't Pendrous' lecturers and tutors concerned by his absence? It is difficult to say. The problem of poor class attendance is now a significant feature of higher education. Once students have paid their fees, many universities implicitly accept they may not attend lectures, especially with online learning platforms available. Couple this with the fact that many students also work part-time jobs, then attendance is going to suffer, no matter how charismatic a professor might be. Furthermore, in light of the massification of student numbers (as cash-strapped universities compete for more students, especially the lucrative international market), Mason Pendrous' absence (or presence) might not have been noticed in a giant lecture hall. Indeed, there's a good chance that after his death many teachers still probably didn't have a clue who he was. That's not their fault – it's simply the nature of the industry today.

3.

Most of those halls of residences lay dormant for months following the Covid-19 pandemic. Initiatives to reactivate campuses have been hampered by a resurgence of the killer-virus. Both staff and students are understandably paranoid. Many prominent academics have already died.[8] And we all know that those calling for a business-as-usual approach won't be the ones on the frontline, walking into overcrowded lecture halls. As I argued earlier, the massive disruption caused by the pandemic revealed fracture lines that were already present in universities, yet hardly ever picked up in management spreadsheets and revenue stream figures.

But here's the truly worrying part. Even if students like Pendrous did seek help, they might very well find staff who are *also* struggling to cope with the pressures of life in the market-led university.

Take the case of 52-year-old Gregory Eells, former executive director of Counselling and Psychological Services at Pennsylvania University.[9] He was a celebrated expert on mental resilience at Cornell University for ten years before moving to his new job. In an interview for the Cornell student magazine, he said, 'I have dedicated over 15 years of my professional career to providing mental health care to thousands of Cornell students through my work in CAPS.'[10] On another occasion Eells remarked, 'all of us will face times when our heart is broken, resilience is about what we do with that. Can we make art with those pieces?'[11]

A press release by university Provost Wendell Pritchett announced that Eells' new role was to 'increase capacity ... decrease the time between a first consultation and a first counselling appointment'.[12]

This was more difficult than Eells had planned. It didn't help that his wife and children hadn't immediately joined him in Philadelphia, so he spent a lot of time alone. Eells' mother remembers long conversations about his demanding job: 'I said, "well, quit." His wife said the same thing ... we are confused. He was the most smiling, upbeat person I have met in my life.'[13]

Gregory Eells committed suicide by jumping from a downtown high-rise building in September 2019. His death was shocking given his occupation ... to prevent students from acts of self-harm. While University of Pennsylvania officials declined to comment, eyebrows were raised about its organisational culture; 14 students had killed themselves since 2014, with families raising serious questions about the college's duty of care. One popular student – Madison Holleran – jumped from the same building complex as Eells back in 2014.[14] Her father said she 'killed herself because she was overwhelmed with schoolwork at UPenn'.[15]

The University of Pennsylvania isn't alone in this regard. Other higher education facilities have become suicide hotspots too, like Bristol University in the UK, with 13 deaths in only a few odd years.[16] In 2016 seven students committed suicide at Columbia University months apart, including a Japanese exchange student who leapt from her dorm window.[17] Universities in South Korea and Hong Kong have suffered similar tragedies.

4.

The UPenn case is unusual for one good reason. If both students and trained professionals employed to counsel them through tough times are jumping to their deaths, then something must be seriously awry. The incident risked becoming a major scandal for officials. However, and more generally speaking, following the obligatory condolences and tributes paid to the deceased, most universities have a well-rehearsed script for diverting attention away from their own problematic cultures. The first is to remind everyone that suicide is a societal problem. Deaths on campus are thus expected given national figures. Rolling averages are useful in this respect because they help smooth out any conspicuous spikes.[18]

This argument was actually perfected over a decade ago by France Telecom. Bad management was connected to 19 suicides and 12 attempts between 2008 and 2009.[19] One employee even lit himself on fire in the carpark. Executives argued that suicide afflicted the country as a whole, not just their firm. The neo-corporate university has adopted the same rhetoric, insisting that modern society is to blame. Just look at the statement issued by the Pro Vice Chancellor for Student Experience after yet another death at Bristol University:

> Like all universities, schools and colleges, we are deeply concerned by the increase of mental health issues amongst our young people nationally. Complex mental health challenges cannot be addressed by universities alone, and we cannot be expected to replace the NHS.[20]

Another argument used by university officials – echoed too in the carefully crafted press release above – taps into the dogma of individualism that is so pervasive today. References to 'underlying mental issues' encourage one to assume that the root cause lies with the student, irrespective of their institutional circumstances. We all know the familiar story: she or he had a family history of depression; had elevated levels of glucocorticoids; struggled with anxiety and anhedonia; was diagnosed with ADHD, etc. From the university's perspective, which is seeking to minimise reputational damage, the refrain represents a 'free pass' card because it's difficult to prove otherwise given the nature of suicide: it patently involves someone with severe psychological issues, no matter how dire their social surroundings may be.

But this formula is too simple. Organisational settings obviously have a substantial effect on our psychological wellbeing, with or without pre-existing conditions.[21] Specific economic characteristics associated with neoliberalisation, especially as it staggers from one crisis to another, are important to note in this respect. For one thing, the normal psychic protections we once relied upon are seriously eroded when the division between self and work, life and labour all but disappear. This is not just about addiction to email and high-tech communication devices, which is certainly ubiquitous in academia. Instead it goes to the heart of the neoclassical vision of what labour intrinsically means. For example, Human Capital Theory was developed by Chicago School economists to demonstrate how human existence is primarily an economic one, no matter where (or when) you are. This includes marriage and all other personal activities. The economy never switches off and nor should you. Contemporary academia is a notorious case in point given how many experience it as a vocational 'calling'. We *are* what we do. We *live* our careers to the point of exhaustion.

The highly interconnected and cognitive nature of economic activity today means that it's often difficult to separate external worries (e.g., meeting a deadline, aggressive hierarchies, demanding workloads, etc.) from internal ones like anxiety and melancholy. Post-industrial institutions are both 'greedy' (*outwardly* absorbing our personal time with ease) and 'leaky' (*inwardly* overcrowding us with their own hang-ups and troubles). It's ironic, but rampant individualism provides little mental self-defence. On the contrary, it allows the crap to flow into us without respite. Consequently, a bullying colleague becomes an inner voice that sneers at us and fuels self-hate. A looming deadline makes you loath the world and the person you've become. Overwork is a sign of your stupidity.

But how does this bad 'external' energy get mysteriously converted into negative 'internal' energy? Why does an unjust social setting induce feelings of worthlessness and auto-belittlement rather than pride, indignation and revolt? Once again, individualisation is central to the problem. Dignity is very difficult to summon when you're isolated in an unfriendly institutional space. Soon you too acquire the 'boss syndrome' and it's always more vindictive when wielded against yourself. If we are treated as non-entities, then perhaps we actually are and then some. If our employer distrusts what they see in us then so should we, perhaps doubly so. In psychotherapeutic terms, the victim seeks to control their humiliation by absorbing the role of the humiliator themselves. It's a coping mechanism that rarely ends well. Power is a crucial part of the puzzle because the old equation still holds: the more someone is subjected to power, the more power*less* they feel, not the opposite. And this slowly chips away at our psychic foundations.

5.

It is disheartening to survey the recent academic suicides that have occurred in the shadow of the corporate university. But I think my theory at least partially explains what's going on. For example, Professor Stefan Grimm was allegedly bullied by superiors at Imperial College when he failed to meet grant income and publication targets.[22] In 2014 he wrote an email to his entire department and set it on a delayed timer. Colleagues only received the message after he had hanged himself at home. The email lambasted his superiors and lamented the fate of the UK university. Grimm also gave a rather sardonic twist to the slogan, 'publish or perish':

> This is not a university anymore but a business with very few up in the hierarchy, like our formidable duo, profiteering and the rest of us are milked for money, be it professors for their grant income or students who pay 100.- pounds just to extend their write-up status ... this leads to an interesting spin to the old saying 'publish or perish'. Here it is 'publish and perish'.[23]

A few years later, father-of-three Malcolm Anderson's 2018 death at Cardiff University rocked the academic community because his work conditions were not that dissimilar to those of many in British higher education.[24] As a lecturer in accounting,

48-year-old Anderson complained to university management about his workload. It was too much and he was struggling with the large classes. According to his wife, Anderson graded exam papers at family events in the weekend to meet deadlines: 'he did tell them. In his appraisals he told them that his workload was massive and it was unmanageable but nothing ever changed.'[25] Anderson's widow continued,

> ... he carried the burden of his work with him. He spent many hours with his personal tutees who would email him day and night. He had a huge pile of exam papers to mark and was often unable to spend time with his family. His commute was a 120-mile round trip and he would often start early at six or seven and work late ... [he] was silently struggling.[26]

Anderson jumped from his university office window. On the day of his death he was responsible for 600 students, frantically preparing lectures and under pressure to finish grading 418 exam scripts. Less than two days after Anderson's suicide, staff received an email at 5.30 pm on Friday notifying them of their workload allocation.[27] Another reminder was sent 7 am Saturday morning.

Death by suicide is relatively uncommon in the neoliberal university. Perhaps a more likely scenario is involuntary death, where the combination of poor wages and micromanagement see the physical organism simply give in. This might sound far-fetched, but what we could term *economic casualties* have been associated with the proletariatisation of academic labour and the unhealthy work habits it can engender. Many universities have cultivated a 'flexible' labour pool in order to be cost-effective. From a managerial standpoint, most of what happens in the university is an *expense*, a drain on finances. Fixed-term contracts offset those costs and allow administrators to allocate work in an on-demand fashion. A short-term view for sure, more akin to the churn-and-burn business

models favoured in retail and hospitality, but popular nevertheless. As a result, the recruitment of adjuncts and casual staff has
burgeoned in recent years, even among elite institutions. In the UK,
for example, 68 per cent of research staff are on fixed-term contracts.
The pressure this places on casual labour in the age of austerity has
ignited a veritable mental health crisis in higher education.[28]

But seasonal staff in US colleges have got it the worst. In 2013,
83-year-old adjunct professor Margaret Mary Vojtko died under
circumstances that were truly frightening and sparked a major
debate about pay and conditions in American higher education.[29]
For 25 years she taught French at Duquesne University, a Catho-
lic-based institution. Vojtko's workload was onerous, including
three classes per semester and two during summer. Even then her
income barely reached US$25,000 with no healthcare benefits. By
comparison, Duquesne's President earned US$700,000 with full
entitlements.

Then Vojtko was diagnosed with cancer and her health dete-
riorated. Soon the medical bills mounted and she was unable to
teach her normal classes. When she was caught napping between
lessons at Duquesne University, Vojtko was marched off the
premises and fired. Soon the medicine and electricity ran out.
Vojtko began working nights at Eat'n Park for extra income. Not
long after she was found unresponsive on her front lawn having
suffered a massive heart attack. A labour lawyer who attended
Vojtko's funeral summed up the situation:

> The funeral Mass for Margaret Mary, a devout Catholic, was
> held at Epiphany Church, only a few blocks from Duquesne.
> The priest who said Mass was from the University of Dayton,
> another Catholic university and my alma mater. Margaret Mary
> was laid out in a simple, cardboard casket devoid of any handles
> for pallbearers – a sad sight, but an honest symbol of what she
> had been reduced to by her ostensibly Catholic employer.[30]

6.

Clearly Vojtko had age working against her. But even younger adjuncts are now meeting a similar fate, like Thea Hunter.[31] She was a gifted black-studies scholar from New York who received a doctorate at Columbia University in 2004. After entering the academic job market Hunter found a tenure-track position at Western Connecticut State University, but the job soon turned sour. Being a black female in a predominantly white institution was difficult. She said someone even mistook her for a janitor when arriving early one morning at the office. Hunter finally quit and took on adjunct teaching as a temporary measure. Being a graduate from a prestigious university like Columbia, she assumed, would mean another tenure-track job was just around the corner.

But it never arrived. Hunter was soon a permanent member of the 'untenured underclass'. In 1969 up to 80 per cent of faculty in American universities were tenured.[32] Today three quarters are now untenured. There's a strong racial dimension too. Between 1993 and 2013 the number of untenured minorities grew by 230 per cent.[33]

Adjunct professors live a stressful and peripatetic life, literally delivering a lecture at one campus, dashing to the carpark and driving to their next 'gig'. This exhausting regime wore down Thea Hunter and her health suffered. She had forfeited health insurance and a reliable pay check after leaving her tenured position. As we saw with Margaret Mary Vojtko, the US is a terrible place to exist if you get ill and cannot afford treatment. Hunter confessed to a close friend in an email,

> I have been saying I am done, emotionally drained and without reserves. There has just been too much going on in my life that has been drawing upon whatever emotional reserves I have. That plus the constant financial crisis that has been my life for years takes its toll.[34]

Her friends noticed a significant change in Hunter's behaviour during this period. She became very withdrawn and secretive. When her health suddenly failed she was unable to afford medical treatment or even basic check-ups. Upon entering New York-Presbyterian Hospital in December 2018 a doctor declared, 'her lungs were full of fluid; her body was full of fluid'.[35] Hunter was suffering from multiple organ failure.

Jim Downs was Hunter's friend from the Columbia days. He was the first to learn of her passing and searched in vain for family members to claim the body. In the end he contacted friends to help pay for transporting Hunter from the hospital to a funeral home. It took three weeks.

7.

In present times, one of the more bewildering chimeras of the human body is its symbolic resonance with radical self-ownership. In reality, of course, the body only does what any society tells it to do. We are all Spinozians in this respect. But capitalist realism continues to prime human beings as discrete economic units, ones that observe strict boundary-lines between them and the world. This artificial fetishisation of the individual is nearly pathological today. Yet it is still difficult to openly confront, particularly within the domain of ethico-political reason: violence the body bears, our society continues to maintain, could never be linked to the peaceable and civil institutions that enframe it. Losers are products of their own making and winners likewise, end of story.

But obviously it isn't the end. The tragedies of Malcolm Anderson, Margaret Mary Vojtko and Thea Hunter are symptoms of a dark totality. Yes, the deaths are exceptional. But I can't help thinking that the same sunless sea soon awaits many others. Bodies hitting the atrium far below? No. Probably something worse.

While the modern university has managed to keep up appearances, pretending to remain that idyllic and gentle institution in the popular imagination, complete with sandstone buildings and Latin mottos, in reality it has become one of the more saturnine zones in the new economic order.

7

High Impact ...

1.

When the 500 pound GBU-12 Paveway II laser-guided bomb left the Saudi jetfighter, it only took a few seconds to hit its target. This turned out to be a family house in Ta'iz, Yemen, in June 2019. A farmer working nearby recalled the scene: 'I heard the plane hovering and I saw the bomb as it dropped towards the house. I was next to the house when the second bomb fell ... and I got down onto the ground.'[1]

In the house a family of six – including a 52-year-old mother and three children, aged twelve, nine and six – were killed instantly. After 15 minutes the Saudi jetfighter returned and bombed the house again. And then once more five days later. There were no military targets in the vicinity, so reports suggested the home had been mistaken for an old Huthi Operations Room a few clicks away. It was destroyed by Coalition Forces in 2016. Regardless, when loved ones arrived to search for survivors, they only found body parts:

> We buried them the same day because they had turned into severed limbs. There were no corpses left to examine. The flesh of this person was mixed with that person. They were wrapped up with blankets and taken away.[2]

The Saudi and Emirati-led war against Yemen has become notorious for the high number of non-combatant deaths. Since the conflict began in 2015, the country has become a killing ground with around 18,000 civilians dying in bombing raids and a resulting famine affecting 17 million Yemenis.[3]

The laser-guided 'precision bomb' that killed the family in Ta'iz was manufactured by US defence contractor Raytheon. American, British and French firms still trade weapons and military equipment worth billions of dollars with Saudi Arabia, even as the atrocities mount up. In August 2018 a laser-guided MK 82 bomb manufactured by Lockheed Martin obliterated a school bus in Northern Yemen, killing 40 small children.[4] UK firm BAE Systems supply Typhoon jet fighters, etc.[5]

Raytheon is the world's third largest defence contractor with US$24 billion in annual sales. Its laser-guided bombs – like the deadly GBU-12 Paveway II laser mentioned above – are a best-seller. The company employs 67,000 workers and is based in Waltham, Massachusetts. It boasts a major training and research partnership with University of Massachusetts Lowell (or UMass Lowell). One project holds pride of place, a 3-D printer that might one day build missiles in the field.[6] However, university researchers mainly work on mundane projects like mathematical modelling and weapons design.[7]

In 2014 the multi-million dollar Raytheon-UMass Lowell Research Institute (RURI) was established to cement the partnership. The facility shares laboratories and classrooms, providing engineering students work experience at Raytheon. The company now employs thousands of university alumni: 'we look forward to bringing the expertise of our top-notch faculty together with researchers from Raytheon', UMass Lowell Chancellor Marty Meehan said, 'this new partnership is just one example of how UMass Lowell is leading the way in collaborating with industry to power innovation and the economy in Massachusetts and beyond'.[8]

2.

The Raytheon-UMass Lowell partnership is an excellent example of a modern university fulfilling a key performance target, one that the sector is now obsessed with: *impact*. That is to say, scholarly activity with influence beyond the so-called ivory tower, delivering practical outcomes for business, contributing to growth and national prosperity.

Demonstrating industry engagement is increasingly treated as a precondition for universities to continue receiving funding, government grants, endowments and meet student 'employability targets'. In England, the REF-2021 links 25 per cent of government funding to impact. This is one reason why universities are now scrambling to cosy-up with necrocapitalist firms like Raytheon, Lockheed Martin and BAE Systems. It ticks the right box and brings in the cash.[9]

But surely the sort of 'impact' that universities are being asked to deliver is of a more positive kind, say, developing an Ebola vaccine or pollution-free technologies? Sure, it could be. But this is a major part of the problem we need to discuss: what 'impact' means is in the eye of the beholder. Unfortunately, this tends to be the all-seeing eye of the neoliberal industrial-complex and its governmental policymakers. In that context, the very notion of impact is predetermined from the start, viewed through the frame of economic instrumentalism, even in cases that might appear innocuous and socially progressive.

Hence my argument: there is no good impact in this market-charged setting because it always turns on fiscal discipline rather than genuinely improving the world. No doubt the two may coincide, but whether that happens or not is largely unimportant within this ideological system. And in cases we would genuinely call pro-social, like advancing antiretroviral therapy for instance, then a different kind of terminology is required.

3.

We must begin by placing the appeal to be 'impactful' within a wider socio-political universe in order to understand its under-lying intent. In their campaign against the university, mainly the public ones, neoliberal governments around the world have casti-gated higher education providers as pointless, elitist and irrelevant … unless they directly contribute to business and society. Most universities don't provide relevant job skills it's argued. Colleges too often add nothing to industry and the taxpayer foots the bill for this luxury.

But no longer cry the pundits. The higher education sector must provide evidence of its impact beyond the ivory tower to remain eligible for funding. This means (according to the American Association of Universities, for example) 'universities serve as economic engines for their communities and regions. In fulfilling their research, education, and service missions, these institutions fuel economic growth and drive innovation'; or (in the UK) universities must have 'an effect on, change or benefit to the economy, society, culture, public policy or services, health, the environment or quality of life, beyond academia' or (to evoke the Australian version) 'the contribution that research makes to the economy, society, environment or culture, beyond the contribution to academic research'.[10]

For the Raytheon-UMass Lowell Research Institute, national defence and homeland security would count as their commercial contribution to US society. Bombs, in other words. And this also enhances the local economy, they'd argue, citing sales, technological innovation and job creation, which are key indicators of relevance.

Precisely here we begin to see the trouble. The commercialisation of academic science and its growing role in corporate R&D began to take shape in the 1970s and 1980s.[11] But it only grew into the powerful pillar of higher education we see today following the triumph of neoclassical economics and the market imperative in universities. According to this discourse, 'the economy' is considered the sole arbiter of social worth, a master signifier that transcends all others values. We can no longer speak about some part of society, be it culture, morality, education or leisure without mentioning its positive or negative impact on growth and prosperity. This is the endpoint of a long linage of neoclassical thought, of course. For instance, in *The Road to Serfdom* in 1944, F.A. Hayek argued that nothing is exempt from the monetary valuation process since it prefigures all other life endeavours. Poetry, aesthetics, art, knowledge for knowledge's sake, 'higher values' associated with empathy and compassion all come with a price-tag. Ultimately, someone has to pay for it.[12] Such is the first principle of neoclassical economics.

It's a conviction that has been applied to higher education with alacrity. Public universities cost money, paid for by ordinary taxpayers. Understanding exactly how academics yield a return on this investment, therefore, should be front and centre. In light of F.A. Hayek's reasoning, we shouldn't be fooled by the references to culture, community and the environment in the above definitions of impact.[13] In the last instance they too are only considered relevant apropos the wider economic climate, with growth, GDP and jobs being the final judge. The discourse of impact is designed to convey the maxim that nothing is free: taxpayers, students and donors want to see their money's worth in real-world terms. More generally, this sentiment has informed the Tories' dark reign in the UK as it dismembered the welfare state. The National Health Service, they insisted, can only be funded if first the national economy is thriving (which it hardly does anymore). The idea of reversing the equation, of course, would be considered blasphemy to most neoliberal zealots.

4.

What we've been speaking of is certainly more pronounced in publicly funded universities, where tertiary institutions are held 'accountable' to taxpayers. But private ones too are subservient to the cult of impact, with donations, endowments and student enrolments contingent on meeting this fundamental objective. Such accountability is frequently fused with an emphasis on technical *solutions*: the university is supposed to supply broader society with answers to grand challenges connected to national security and war, but also poverty, climate change, job growth and other pressing issues. The agenda transforms scholarly institutions into a managerial space, since supplying mechanical solutions is a primary characteristic of the technocratic mindset, something Deloitte consultants specialise in, where delicate ethical situations, for instance, are reformulated into simple apolitical problems.

But isn't a touch of humiliation involved here also? Many of the problems that universities are being called upon to solve were produced by global corporate capitalism, a system that hasn't exactly been an ally of higher education of late, especially concerning tax revenues and public spending. One might ask why it's now the university's responsibility to worry about climate change and poverty-related diseases when we ought to be turning the spotlight on the purveyors of capitalism itself. During the Covid-19 pandemic, for example, the task of reskilling the workforce in order to kick-start the economy fell on universities, not the large corporations that terminated those jobs in the first place.

In any case, when this impact agenda sees higher education contributing to destructive mining practices like fracking (dubbed 'frackademia' in the US) or the military machine, helping to leave large bomb craters where family homes once stood, it's unsurprising that some academics feel troubled.[14] Who wants to work for an institution that's implicated in the killing of innocent youngsters? In March 2019 concerned faculty held a protest about Raytheon at the UMass Lowell's recruitment fair, stating that:

> Anyone who knows anything of this vile company should be absolutely disgusted to know that we as a university collaborate with them. We should be human enough to stand up against their war crimes and, if not demand the perpetrators be held responsible for these actions, at least not want them to profit off the thousands of dead children that have been killed and the many more that will be killed by these monstrous institutions.[15]

Similar demonstrations have been organised by staff and students at MIT, Northwestern, Cal Poly and other institutions around the world. Students in Australia held a 'Books not Bombs' protest against Adelaide University's partnership with Lockheed Martin. It's not surprising then that some universities (along with their powerful corporate and state partners) attempt to give these otherwise disturbing arrangements an ethical gloss. For example, beginning in 2003, Bentley University (Waltham, Massachusetts) sponsors the 'Raytheon Lectureship in Business Ethics', a series of invited talks about responsible business practices.[16] According to the website, 'Raytheon believes in a values-based ethics program, and we believe in the value of ethics education.' Tell that to the Yemenis grieving their loved ones.

5.

The trouble with this interpretation of impact is not just ethical, however: if universities stopped including weapons manufacturers and oil/gas in their 'impact partnerships', the tensions this discourse contains would not magically disappear. It's the injunction to be socially useful and instrumental from a utilitarian viewpoint, even if genuinely principled (unlike Raytheon's cynical evocation of ethics) that remains problematic.

I'm not talking about *social emergency* cases like discovering a cure for a killer strain of influenza or trigeminal neuralgia. Medical science should seek swift and practical solutions for sure. No, I'm referring to the broader political attempt to cajole universities – including geography, law and drama departments – into becoming pragmatic handmaidens of industry and society, in spirit if not deed.

In the same vein, some academics have jumped on the impact bandwagon, using leftish-sounding 'public intellectual' arguments to cloak a rather reactionary stance. For example, in their essay 'Prof, No One Is Reading You', Asit Biswas and Julian Kirchherr rebuke social science scholars for not being more relevant and keener participants in public debate.[17] According to them, academic journal articles are packed with 'incomprehensible jargon and the sheer volume and lengths of papers (often unnecessary!) would still prevent practitioners (including journalists) from reading and understanding them'.

Their solution is to make it mandatory for researchers to ditch the jargon, talk to the media and assist practitioners in the real world. Academics begin to look like management consultants with an overactive Twitter account.[18] One wonders if Biswas and Kirchherr had clearly thought through the full implications of these recommendations. My guess is not. So you're studying the stagecraft of fifteenth century Florentine theatre? Forget it buddy, totally irrelevant in today's business environment and no one understands the lingo anyway. Isn't this precisely how universities die?

In certain disciplines like criminology and economics, the problem is precisely opposite to the one posed by Biswas and Kirchherr: what if too many people, especially among the ruling classes, *are* actually reading the Prof? Sometimes academics can get things very wrong, particularly in the realm of socio-economic policy. For example, the decade-long reign of austerity (high taxes and low public spending) after the global financial crisis was meant to jump-start growth. Governments around the world flocked to Carmen Reinhart and Kenneth Rogoff's 2010 paper explaining why in the *American Economic Review*.[19] The authors argued that average economic growth drops to –0.1 per cent when debt reaches 90 per cent of GDP. Hence the massive cuts to social spending in the Western world designed to mitigate the credit crunch. PhD student Thomas Herndon and his supervisors later looked at the Excel spreadsheet used to make this calculation and discovered basic errors.[20] When corrected it turned out that growth hovered around 2.2 per cent when debt reached 90 per cent, not greatly different to lower GDP/debt ratios. Oops.

Or take the infamous 'Broken Windows Theory' popularised by Harvard University academics James Wilson and George Kelling.[21] If minor misdemeanours go unpunished, they suggested, more serious crime will be encouraged over time in a cascading fashion. So municipal leaders had police clampdown on trivial infringements and implement a zero-tolerance policy. Even a broken car taillight provoked harsh treatment from law enforcement officers. The inevitable then happened, including racial profiling and intrusive stop-and-search campaigns in New York, Baltimore and other major cities.[22] The #blacklivesmatter movement and murder of George Floyd revealed one potential outcome of this errant theory when put into practice.

6.

For all but the elite universities today, the impact agenda has drastically narrowed the scope of desirable scholarship, with disciplines considered more practical to industry judged superior: namely, STEM subjects (science, technology, engineering and mathematics), with the addition of medicine when appropriate. In this new academic environ, even subject areas once considered too vocational for universities – business education, for example – now stand outside the tent when it comes to the most robust drivers of impact in tertiary education. Hence why business schools tend to be utilised more as 'cash cows' than legitimate areas of research, a production-line for processing innumerable international students. This in turn permits the cross-subsidisation of industry-relevant research, like engineering and computer science.

The big loser in this high impact culture are the humanities, of course. Their funding has dwindled, leaving English, classics and cultural studies little more than empty husks. Academic life has become grim as a vast number of jobs evaporated, making way for STEM subjects instead.[23] Stanley Fish, 1980s icon of cultural studies, recently wrote a depressing article about this.[24] In terms of applied relevance, he remarks, the humanities has little to offer. Indeed, 'there is no generalizable benefit to having led a life centred on great texts'. Fish concludes on an even gloomier note, 'alas, there will be no turn at the end of this essay to a solution everyone else has missed ... I can't think of a plan that would return the humanities to the prominence they once enjoyed.'

Fish is correct only if we adopt a very limited, Rupert Murdoch-like view of impact, of course, which is part of his point. If we take a wider perspective, the humanities remain relevant on an utmost pragmatic level. Take the example of philosophy. We live in a world where the exact meaning of good and evil, right and wrong, just and unjust are contested more now than ever. Deep thinking is required to offer precise definitions and their implications, otherwise it will be left to dim-witted politicians to decide for us. Yes, the concrete utility gleaned from reflecting on these issues falls outside the neoliberal impact matrix, but perhaps that was the plan all along. Don't get me wrong. There are problems that need little philosophical reflection, like building bridges or mending a broken arm. But when it comes to arguments about the desirability of free markets, animal testing and who should live or die when a pandemic lays civilisation low, philosophical thought is essential. The current impact agenda registers none of this.

Stanley Fish and his colleagues are in the twilight of their careers. Therefore, in order to get a proper feel for what's going on in the humanities we should ask the grad students who were promised jobs in these vanishing disciplines. There is no shortage of online advice from those who've been burnt. Take the author of this article, 'Getting a Literature Ph.D. Will Turn You Into an Emotional Trainwreck, Not a Professor':

> I now realize graduate school was a terrible idea because the full-time, tenure-track literature professorship is extinct. After four years of trying, I've finally gotten it through my thick head that I will not get a job ... don't do it, just don't.[25]

But perhaps Andrew Kay's piece about attending the Modern Language Association conference in Chicago is definitive in this regard.[26] He graduated with a PhD in English a few years back but couldn't find university employment. There weren't any jobs. So spurred on by morbid curiosity and reckless quantities of Scotch whisky, Kay spent a hilarious few days at the convention to see how the discipline was coping with its impending extinction. The attendees – in much diminished numbers compared to 'Peak English' times in the 1970s – mostly seemed blissfully unaware of the disaster approaching.[27] However, after being cornered by Kay in a late-night hotel bar some conference-goers finally admitted things weren't looking good. Years of aggressive downsizing in the name of social utility meant that scholars in areas like French Theory, early Twentieth Century Latin American literature and Spanish baroque style prose were now an endangered species.

7.

Something radically changes the nature of scientific inquiry more generally in this 'high impact' setting. The expectation of direct and measurable relevance, usually bureaucratically monitored on a continuous basis, often doesn't take into consideration how proper research is conducted.

Much of the time, breakthroughs (both large and small) are not accomplished with this overt instrumentality in mind. That's true even of applied research fields that are presumed to exemplify practical knowledge.[28] A range of very useful innovations were created under conditions that were intrinsically motivating (driven by internal satisfaction, curiosity, adventure, fun, etc.) rather than compelled by carrot and sticks.[29] Oftentimes discoveries are made by chance (e.g., penicillin, pacemakers, insulin, safety glass, radio-activity, etc.). Others take years of tinkering, with many dead ends and false starts along the way (e.g., television, monoclonal anti-bodies for cancer treatment, etc.). New ideas in one industry may find successful dissemination in very different social fields (like NASA's incredible miniaturisation of computer screens in the 1960s and their later use in mobile phone technology).

I do not want to idealise any of this. Of course profit-maximising businesses have combined inventive inspiration and extrinsic rewards, with some successful outcomes. But what the corporate world (and increasingly the state apparatus) excels in is *application* and *commercialisation*. And this points to an even more serious issue. We need to realise that impact is a *two-way* process. When universities seek industry relevance, it shouldn't be surprising that industry soon impacts on universities too, changing their institutional logic in noticeable ways. Here we can recall the University of Utah example discussed by Jennifer Washburn.[30] When researchers discovered a chromosome 17 gene linked to hereditary breast cancer (BRCA1), they didn't make it freely available to fellow scientists in other universities or medical schools. Instead the breakthrough was quickly patented and licensed to Myriad Genetics, Inc. Money was to be made after all and it didn't seem to matter that the initial research had been funded by the public system.

This doxa of utility has yet another troubling consequence concerning the university labour process. Whether intentionally or not, it sends a strong message to academics, befitting of insecure workers in an era of market discipline: how do *you* contribute to business and society? And perhaps more incisively, exactly how have you added value to your place of employment? When pragmatism is symbolically institutionalised in this fashion it puts faculty on the back foot, in a position where they must prove their worth, both to university management and themselves. In other words, it tips the power balance in favour of employers. As I mentioned at the beginning of this chapter, it isn't coincidental that the impact agenda appeared precisely when models from neoclassical economics proliferated in higher education. There is no such thing as a free lunch. You must demonstrate your practical worth to an organisation (or 'Employee Corporate Value Proposition') in order to be counted a valuable member of its community. The immense pressure on academics to apply for external grants at the moment – particularly those linked to business and industry – is part of this.

8.

There's one final question we must discuss in relation to impact before drawing some brief conclusions. What about academics who are highly critical of patriarchy, income inequality, racism, environmental degradation and authoritarian capitalism? If they want to see society change for the better, shouldn't they be doing more than just writing about it? Yes, I think so. A certain activism within and beyond the university, as Jodi Dean has recently argued, is essential in today's political climate, which promises to plumb new lows in the coming years.[31]

However, this stance is not without its own ideological risks and dangers.

As 'anti-expert' populism took off, critical intellectuals have found themselves in a hopeless double-bind. On the one hand, they're chastised for not being real-world enough, cloistered in their ivory towers and reading too many books. On the other, if critical academics do speak out about current affairs they're castigated as elitist snobs, as the vilifying debates around Brexit, Trump, war in the Middle East, immigration and climate change amply illustrate.[32]

But I don't think we can simply commandeer the discourse of 'impact' (as defined in this chapter) and steer it towards emancipatory ends. This is an important point. In one of the last essays written before his death in 1969, T.W. Adorno responded to the repudiation of critical theory by student demonstrators during the May '68 uprisings. They argued that Adorno and several other members of the Frankfurt School were not revolutionaries at all but fixtures of the establishment, 'armchair rebels' as revealed by their aversion to civil disobedience.

There's some truth to the charge of hypocrisy. Adorno famously called the police when strikers occupied his lecture hall. Nevertheless, it troubled the philosopher. In an essay called 'Resignation', Adorno admits that he 'does not want to deny the element of subjective weakness that clings to the narrow focus on theory'.[33] Yet non-participation in street protests shouldn't automatically be equated with resignation or the belief that transformative change is unrealistic. That would be too dualistic, Adorno avers. Such a concatenation could easily morph into a prohibition against philosophical thought per se, yielding to a faith in action that believes doing *anything* is preferable to thinking. The problem is that 'anything' can possibly result in nothing or worse. Action and the void discover their Archimedean point therein. So if rebellion is impelled by the longing to escape our hegemonic enclosure, from power relations that feel absurd and yet impervious to practical refusal, then philosophical reflection is crucial for breaking the deadlock.[34] Otherwise, duplicating the neoliberal impact agenda on the left would risk seeing patient learning, study and thinking demoted yet again. And they remain our only hope.

Few would interpret UMass Lowell's version of impact in a cheerful light. And military partnerships and weapons design are only the tip of the iceberg. Just think of university involvement in developing artificial intelligence (AI) surveillance for authoritarian regimes, animal testing collaborations with private labs and joint projects with big tobacco companies. But even when turned to progressive ends, the impact narrative conveys a bureaucratic instrumentalisation of knowledge that is dangerous. How so? Because it's symptomatic of a very specific variant of capitalist realism. The ultimate aim is to move academics into the domain of performativity, a ceremony of action that's more circular than linear. Any free university in the future would therefore need to recover the entire meaning of efficacy and reverse its reduction to the most ethereal notion of all ... *relevance*.

8

The Academic Star-Complex

1.

Witnessing Slovenian bestselling Marxist Slavoj Žižek give a talk is something to behold. The press doesn't call him the 'Elvis of Cultural Theory' and a 'Rockstar Academic' for nothing. I've been lucky enough to see him several times, but a 2009 conference in London stands out. A large audience filed into the London auditorium to see the intellectual superstar. He delivered an animated speech. Some years later Žižek-mania reached new heights when he teamed up with right-wing psychologist Jordan Peterson, another intellectual heavyweight on the lecture circuit. Peterson's book *12 Rules for Life* is a paean for angry white men who think capitalism is hardwired into our DNA and 'Cultural Marxism' the root of all evil. The event was advertised as the 'debate of the century' and bootleg tickets fetched US$1500 on eBay. Unfortunately, many were seriously underwhelmed by the debate. Two old men rambling through a disjointed exchange, finally agreeing that the contemporary political left is indeed shit.

Seldom do academics become stars like Žižek and Peterson, where the general public recognises them and they feature regularly in the media. The notion of the 'public intellectual', of course, has been around for years and can be traced back to the Dreyfus Affair.[1] In this tradition we may also think of Jean-Paul Sartre, Susan Sontag, James Baldwin and Angela Davis among others as iconic intellectuals, gaining prominence because they spoke out on controversial topics and got into hot water as a result (e.g., Bertrand Russell famously served jail-time as a conscientious objector). However, these academics, who often fled the university as soon as they could, found fame as a secondary effect of their activities. Chasing recognition wasn't their primary objective, on the contrary.

The widespread popularity of Michel Foucault in the 1970s and early 1980s could be identified as a transitional point. A 1981

Time Magazine feature on the French philosopher spoke of over-flowing lecture halls and mesmerised students, 'Foucault exerts a strange fascination on a growing cult of students.'[2] It is perhaps telling that a year or so before this *Time Magazine* profile, Foucault had largely abandoned his left-wing agenda and was immersing himself in neoclassical economics instead, particularly theories about how people invest in themselves qua 'human capital'. As the market price of *his* human capital was peaking, 'Saint Foucault' (as some deified him) was clearly enjoying the blandishments of notoriety.

Pierre Bourdieu's *Homo Academicus* provides a unique account of French academic stardom during this period.[3] Derrida, Foucault and Althusser (there were unfortunately few women in this clique), 'not to mention more minor prophets', had a tenuous relationship with the traditional French university.[4] They were not establishment figures by any means and worked on the margins, permitting them to cultivate an aura of independent genius, floating intellectuals who stood in judgement with superior observational powers. While flourishing beyond the university like businessmen, Bourdieu notes how French intellectuals courted its institutional power nevertheless, especially as their reputations grew in the US. Colleges there scrambled to invite Derrida, Foucault and others to their campuses, drawing large crowds at speaking events.

Meanwhile in France, these stars of the 'intellectual hit parade', as Bourdieu referred to them, were soon overshadowed by the 'nouveaux philosophes' in the early 1980s, with figures like Raymond Aaron, Bernard-Henri Lévy and André Glucksmann now hogging the limelight. Their anti-Marxism was a curious contrast to the Sartrean public intellectual. It heralded a new era of academic fame, one that was flashy, hip and rich, populated with made-for-television philosophers or '*les* fast-thinkers'.[5] At any rate, this ambitious careerism among the French intelligentsia, Bourdieu wryly observes, appears to have taken more than a few cues from the discourse of entrepreneurship that was busy redefining the Western world at the time.[6]

2.

Academic celebrity has moved on considerably since the heady days of Michel Foucault. Media and money have entered the picture to a greater extent. Fame is no longer a by-product of intellectual praxis but his or her primary *raison d'être*. This is very different to ordinary professional success, although the two can overlap in the current academic marketplace. One may find some very talented law scholars and geneticists who are not 'stars' in this sense. Instead we're interested in academics who seek to commodify their expertise and promote themselves through any means possible. They have literary agents telling them how wonderful they are. A personal webpage and tailored Twitter account. They appear regularly on the international speaking circuit, where a small fortune can be made. Speaker's fees in the age of online media forums (e.g., TED Talks, Google Talks and the Institute of Art and Ideas) have transformed academic celebrity into a lucrative business model. Trade publishers also encourage constant visibility, disseminating their author's name and face far and wide. Malcom Gladwell and Germaine Greer subsequently become universal cultural reference points, no matter how crude their ideas may be.

Gladwell and Greer, however, are in the upper echelon of the pack, members of a small coterie. What we could call second-tier academic stars or 'starlets' are not household names nor feature in *Time Magazine*, but they're still well known in their respective fields and enjoy kudos beyond the typical scholar. Starlets are business school academics, psychologists, biologists and computer engineers who can't quite break free from the university, so attempt to cultivate brand recognition to advance their careers within it. To repeat, what distinguishes an otherwise successful professor

115

from an academic starlet is this: the latter actively manages their public profile in an aggressive manner, shamelessly building social networks, media contacts and so on. They eagerly agree to television interviews and write opinion pieces on *any* topic whatsoever since being seen (rather than the ideas themselves) is what matters the most.

Famous academics can leverage their reputation on the job market and obtain positions at more prestigious universities, with considerably higher incomes as a result. Universities love academic starlets too. While seeking attention they automatically publicise the institution, like walking billboards. Importantly, starlets serve an indirect power function. Universities realise they can help break down solidary among the faculty, displacing management-labour tensions onto the scholarly community itself as academics vie with each other for pole position. The presence of a few starlets among the faculty perpetuates the mythos of the intellectual virtuoso, a scholar who is superior to the rest, attracts more grant money and deserves higher rewards. With the assistance of starlets, the institutional terrain can now be redrawn as a competitive *game*, where winners and losers are clearly demarcated.

3.

The commercialisation of universities has been a significant driver of the academic star-complex. The individualism that arises tends to be underwritten by narcissistic tendencies, with an added touch of insecurity and envy. Academics are encouraged to feel both self-important and yet constantly afraid of being outdone or over-shadowed by rivals. Stanford University professor David Labaree argues that this reflects fundamental changes in how academics are governed in the Edu-Factory.[7] Because most scholars are intrinsically committed to their work, the university finds it difficult to rely on financial incentives alone. Most of us don't become academics to obtain more power and money. Our occupational rewards stem from qualities inherent to the craft of scholarship itself, structured around a shared community of practice rather than status symbols bestowed by authority.

As a result, higher education needed to deploy an alternative motivational matrix, one more in tune with the possessive individualism pervading late capitalism as a whole. The beauty of the new approach is this: no one had to force academics to accept it. Instead the university simply massaged their ambition and pride, nudging them towards the highly competitive profession we see today. Consequently, as Labaree remarks, 'we want to be recognised for our academic accomplishments by earning our own little pieces of fame. So we work assiduously to accumulate a set of merit badges over the course of our careers, which we then proudly display on our CVs.'[8] Hence the birth of a rather pathetic celebrity culture in higher education. It then isn't long before professional jealously enters the picture, fomenting a toxic mix of self-doubt and wanton ambition. Gossip and backstabbing come next, etc.

This is hardly a sound basis for collegial goodwill and knowledge sharing, attributes long considered essential to the scientific endeavour. What sociologist Robert Merton once called the 'communism of science', for example, with its spirit of open collaboration, seems positively antediluvian in this context.[9]

What I find interesting is how academic agency has been central for realising this new culture of individualism. Scholars themselves have actively invested in the game, a seductive but ultimately unforgiving *illusio*, without fully appreciating how the odds of them becoming famous are ridiculously low. Indeed, to boost the veneration of starlets in the neoliberal university, a clear counterpoint was created: namely, the nobodies. So a likely outcome of playing this game is widespread non-stardom, which is very different to 'anti-stardom' since the former still has a stake in the game. My point is this. The university has certainly innovated in the use of coercive management techniques and market logics to regulate its workforce. But academics aren't entirely innocent either. Many have signed a Faustian-pack with the new order in the hope of finding glory or at least preferential treatment.

But what about merit? Aren't some academics simply better than others, superior talent who ought to be rewarded accordingly? Sure, there are some great thinkers, scientists and scholars around, like Noam Chomsky, Mary Beard and Fred Moten who deserve all the attention they receive. But they're not part of this. The celebrity complex I'm interested in involves a more mundane group of academics who strive to transform merit into public recognition, sometimes desperately so. Networking and self-promotion is their forte, exploiting every available avenue to heighten their public profile, frequently saturating Facebook and Twitter with their latest achievements and so forth.

4.

If reaching the desired level of fame proves difficult for aspiring academic starlets, then help can be found. A recent paper entitled 'Three Ways to Become an Academic Superstar' uses quantitative modelling to isolate the fame variables at play.[10] This is no hoax article. Fame is conceptualised as an information exchange problem. The rationale runs like this. Some scientists and scholars gain more attention in the community than others because people read them more. The question of *why* (or content) is left to one side. If an academic has better networks and connections in the academy, citation levels will accordingly be higher. Given the algebraic nature of the analysis, a succinct Bayesian formula is posited for those wishing to figure out how to become a superstar. It reads as follows:

$$p = \alpha^n \varepsilon / \beta^n (1-\varepsilon) + \alpha^n \varepsilon$$

If you're perplexed like me, don't worry. Rather than rely on complicated mathematics to discover the secret to academic fame, other analysts have studied the habits of celebrity role-models instead. Adam Grant, a professor at the Wharton Business School, is widely considered one. He is the subject of online blogs like 'The Writing Strategy of a Superstar Scholar'.[11] Grant's profile is also discussed in Cal Newport's *Deep Work*.[12] So what makes Grant so special? He became a distinguished professor in his 30s. His articles are some of the most cited in business studies. He is winner of numerous teaching awards. Grant has even written a bestselling business book and co-authored another with famed Facebook COO Sheryl Sandberg. And finally, Grant has an impressive media presence, including TED Talks and op-eds in the *New York Times*, all proudly itemised on his website. It seems that Grant knows he's famous and is happy to offer tips for those who aspire to follow in his footsteps.

As Grant notes in his own contribution to pop-management – *Originals: How Non-Conformists Move the World* – one major component of success is sheer volume. Produce a lot and hope for the best: 'the most predictable path to quality is quantity – but many people fail to achieve originality because they develop one or two ideas – then obsessively refine them trying to reach some kind of perfection'.[13] Grant recommends writing on an industrial scale, often working on many projects at once. This takes a lot of focused time, of course, which is another part of Grant's formula. As Cal Newport notes, 'Grant alternates between periods where his door is open to students and colleagues, and periods where he isolates himself to focus completely and without distraction on a single research task.'[14] Another star equation is presented to help readers imitate Grant's work ethic:

High-Quality Work Produced = (Time Spent) x (Intensity of Focus)[15]

Missing from this formula are the potential hidden costs that this fame-building tactic may involve. One has to ask: who's picking up Grant's teaching and service duties while he's locked away working on the next bestseller? How many adjuncts are required to cocoon him from the daily grind of university life? And what kind of faculty culture ensues when a celebrity is in their midst? Given the mystique of individualism that surrounds academic starlets like Adam Grant, such questions are hardly ever addressed, of course.

5.

We can safely posit three character-types that emerge from the academic star-complex in the neoliberal university. The *academic starlet* (who rides a wave of popularity and prominence, publishes innumerable articles in 'top' journals and are minor celebrities within their scholarly community), the *wannabe starlet* (who ambitiously strives to reach academic celebrity status) and the *failed starlet* (who's bid for fame was unsuccessful). Importantly, all three characters are part of the same social field.

Let us begin with the academic starlet.

Although she or he will never be the next Carlo Rovelli or Yuval Noah Harari, they have nevertheless achieved a high degree of visibility among their peer group and receive regular media and keynote invitations. This profile is then leveraged to land professorial posts at prestigious universities and negotiate reduced teaching and/or service responsibilities. As noted with business school starlet Adam Grant, a major element of success is ring-fencing the time to write: 'within the year, he stacks his teaching into the Fall semester, during which he can turn all of his attention to teaching well and being available to his students. By batching his teaching in the Fall, Grant can turn his attention fully to research in the spring and summer.'[16]

As I see it, the strategy of 'batching' can only work if an army of flexible adjuncts are waiting to pick up the slack elsewhere in the institution. Terry McGlyn, a biology professor at California State University-Dominguez Hills, mentions this in his field. Even non-star tenured professors benefit from the one-sided relationship that adjunctification helps shore up in American colleges. As he remarks, 'full professors benefit from the exploitation of non-tenure-track instructors. Every semester, some of the units that I would otherwise teach are reassigned to those instructors, who are compensated at a rate lower than I am.'[17]

This could explain why universities are willing to pay top dollar for academic celebrities. In the shadow of the star-complex employers can more easily deploy superexploitative management systems for everyone else. *You* are not a star ... so get to work! Authoritarianism tends to prevail wherever academic starlets gain a foothold. An anonymous PhD biochemistry student in the UK recently wrote a scathing indictment of his/her Principal Investigator (or PI) for this very reason: 'playing to the camera' was more important for this celebrity-boss than laboratory work.[18] On the rare occasions she or he made an appearance, 'their treatment of laboratory members was terrible ... these are the eminent scientists you hear about, those who have made such sweeping discoveries that they now consider themselves too superior for even their own laboratory members. They might enter their own laboratory once a month for five minutes or so.'

6.

Academic starlets negatively affect their organisations in other ways, particularly the career psychopathy they inspire in peers and junior academics. Circling around the starlet and intently studying their methods are *wannabe academic starlets*, the second character-type manufactured by the university fame industry. For them, becoming the next Clayton Christensen or Naomi Klein is their singular life-purpose and they will do almost anything to get there. Wannabe academic starlets invariably view the world in a highly instrumental manner. They think to themselves: contemporary academia has presented me with these rules of the game (e.g., publish or perish, citation impact scores, 'top' journals, grant applications, etc.) and I'm going to win at any cost. Meeting a wannabe starlet at a conference is like running into a walking CV. They only talk about themselves and their latest accolades. The more cunning variety will feign informality to gain favour with the big cheese.

This ambition can be so strong that wannabe starlets are sometimes tempted to bend or even break the rules to become famous. Consider the 1999 gene therapy experiments conducted at the University of Pennsylvania, which killed 18-year-old Jesse Gelsinger.[19] An investigation found, 'financial conflicts of interest, combined with the desire to be heroes drove the researchers there to rush human trials of gene therapy'.[20] Similarly, the international medical community was stunned when Chinese biophysicist Associate Professor He Jiankui announced he had genetically edited twin baby girls, using CRISPR-Cas9 technology to modify the CCR5 gene. Most worryingly, he was no rogue scientist. As one commentator remarked, 'it's important to recognize that this person trained at important US institutions and is a product of mainstream science'.[21] It was later revealed that He Jiankui was gunning for a Nobel Prize. *Time Magazine* eventually did name him in their 2018 '100 Most Influential People List', but not for honourable reasons. Experiments conducted by Dr He Jiankui 'will likely be remembered as one of the most shocking misapplications of any scientific tool in our history'.[22] As world condemnation grew, Southern University of Science and Technology terminated his contract. In December 2019 he was finally charged and jailed for three years.

This brings us to the third character-type produced by the academic star-complex, *failed academic starlets*. They have spent years striving to become famous in their field, and for some reason just couldn't make it. Once again we must look at the system rather than the individual, one that is rigged to produce a limited number of winners and define the majority as mediocre. As David

Labaree puts it, 'dashed dreams are the norm for large numbers of actors. This can leave a lot of bitter people occupying the middle and lower tiers of the system, and it can saddle students with professors who would really rather be somewhere else.'[23]

A humiliating fate awaits many failed starlets. They might find themselves doing the drudge work for elite performers, including heavy teaching loads and service duties. An element of resentment inevitably taints their occupational experience.[24] Somewhat strangely, however, many failed academic starlets continue to exhibit an internalisation of the ideology of celebrity even after it has shot them down in flames. Indeed, their failure may forge a *greater* attachment to the star-complex, only this time through the bonds of bitterness. That's why we must still consider failed starlets as an integral part of the celebrity-machine, as opposed to those who reject the game altogether.

While most failed academic starlets remain harmless, retreating into the shadows of mass academia, some decide to enter middle-management instead. Given the aforementioned umbrage, this can spell trouble for those under their charge. These failed starlets often seek revenge and can easily become Hitler-like taskmasters in the process. Successful starlets are seldom their targets because the university power hierarchy protects its most prized assets. So they go after more accessible prey instead, ordinary faculty who are simply getting on with their jobs. Avoiding these angry bureaucrats is an unwritten rule in the neoliberal university today.

7.

When examining the anthropological structure of academic celebrity we must also consider the role of pot luck, being in the right place at the right time. 'Chance' is a dirty word in the neoliberal idiom because it undermines the idea that success and wealth are the product of hard work alone. *Homo economicus* is self-made and thus entirely responsible for his or her fortunes …

and misfortunes. This belief in merit is very robust in academia too, notwithstanding the fact that it clearly favours people from certain socio-economic backgrounds over others. Like chance, the word 'class' is also hardly ever mentioned in the corridors of academe.[25]

So can academic celebrity occur more or less randomly? Yes, more than you might think. One study found that the difference between competence and luck when explaining academic fame was fairly marginal.[26] After surveying citation patterns and social networks, the results were 'consistent with a view on which academic superstars are highly competent academics, but also with a view on which superstars arise primarily due to luck ... it is impossible to tell whether most superstars are in fact competent or lucky'.

One reason for this might be found in the entertainment industry more generally, where popular appeal is notoriously fickle and impossible to predict. Skill and talent are obviously important (most of the time at least), but clearly not the only factor leading to stardom. Whether one becomes the next Ed Sheeran or Ariana Grande is something of a gamble. When it comes to the star power of academics, however, we'd also have to add class background to the mix. Publishing op-eds in the *New York Times* or essays in the *London Review of Books* nearly always reflects the quality of your connections. Generally those with friends in high places are courted by Random House. Competence and skill aren't enough. Success in the academic star-complex is, therefore, probably the outcome of extant social capital (class background, etc.), merit (up to a point) and random luck.

Within the bounds of the neo-corporate university, gaining partial exemption from its disciplinarian rules and responsibilities seems to be the central reason academics seek fame. But in doing so they indirectly valorise and affirm the negative mainstays of neoliberal higher education more generally. Participation in the academic star-complex is therefore problematic from an ethico-political standpoint. There's good reason why successful stars are almost always politically *conservative* today. That critical philosopher and academic star Judith Butler, for example, donated funds to Kamala Harris' campaign rather than Bernie Sanders in the 2019 democratic primaries is hardly surprising.[27] While the contemporary university has generated some famous talking heads on a range of pressing topics, it hasn't produced an intellectual willing to put everything on the line for years. Attachment to the star-complex makes that too risky. In many ways, the academic fame industry signals the death of the 'public intellectual' as far as modern higher education is concerned at least.

9

Student Hellscapes

1.

In 1968 the neoconservative economist James M. Buchanan finally snapped. The object of his ire were protesting students in the nation's universities as the US military escalated its involvement in Vietnam. Buchanan won the Nobel Prize for his work in Public Choice Theory, a framework that modelled government bureaucrats as rational utility-maximisers. Public servants conceal their greed behind a cloak of civic beneficence, he argued. By exposing them to market forces and flushing them out, a level playing field could prevail and private enterprise might get a better deal. Buchanan was a staunch advocate of small government and had close ties with the Chicago School of Economics, where he took his PhD under Frank Knight, the school's founder.

The late 1960s counterculture absolutely horrified Buchanan. Campus militancy was especially disturbing as rebellious youth destroyed university property and openly smoked weed. While Buchanan was working at UCLA, a bomb was found near his building during a dispute with the Black Student Union. That's when Buchanan wrote a book called *Academia in Anarchy*, published in 1970 with Nicos E. Devletoglou.[1] It was dedicated to 'The Taxpayer' and opened with a quote by Richard Nixon about law and order. The book's thesis was radical. The biggest problem with US college education is that citizens get it for *free*, subsidised by taxpayers. Students naturally squander this resource, having no appreciation of its true value. Buchanan describes youths enjoying campus life as if it was a 'LSD trip'. In the absence of tuition fees,

> ... the student will treat the university, its faculty, and its facilities as if little or no scarcity values attaches to them. He will use these precisely as he would use a good that is, in effect, 'free' in the economic sense of the term. There is no incentive for the student to avoid wastage of scarce resources. He has no conception, individually, that costs are involved at all. Is it to be wondered that he treats the whole university setting with disrespect or even with contempt?[2]

If they had to pay for their degrees, as then California Governor Ronald Reagan was also campaigning for, then consumers would realise the real worth of higher education.[3] It's the individual him or herself, Buchanan continued, who benefits from their education in terms of future earnings. So why should anyone else foot the bill? University is no 'gift' Buchanan vehemently spat from the pages. Most importantly, market discipline would finally end the student protests debasing American campuses.

2.

With the help of Margaret Thatcher and Ronald Reagan, these once extreme ideas eventually became mainstream policy. A major consequence today, of course, is the student debt crisis. Federal loans in the US have reached epic proportions, hovering around US$1.6 trillion in 2019.[4] That's an increase of US$61 billion since 2017 and represents 7.5 per cent of GDP.

We can disaggregate these figures to reveal even more troubling trends. Between 1990 and 2018 annual undergraduate tuition fees rose from US$3000 to US$10,000 in public universities and US$15,000 to US$35,000 in private ones.[5] 2.8 million Americans owe US$100,000 or more.[6] In 2018 there were over one hundred individuals owing more than US$1 million.[7] It's estimated that 40 per cent of student loan holders will default by 2030.[8] 3 million people over the age of 60 are saddled with unpaid loans, totalling around US$86 billion.[9] Following graduation, when asked whether they thought their degree was worth it, 21 per cent of millennials said 'definitely not' and 23 per cent replied 'probably not'.[10] This debt mountain has a racial dimension too, affecting black Americans more severely. They default five times more than their white counterparts.[11]

The hardship this debt-sentence inflicts on individuals can be disturbing. In the context of the 2008 recession and the US cost of living crisis, student loans have taken on a rather morbid logic. According to a recent survey, one in 15 borrowers have considered suicide because of their college debt.[12] It was also found that

- 53 per cent of high debt student loan borrowers have experienced depression because of their debt.
- Nine in ten borrowers experienced significant anxiety due to their loan burden.
- One in eleven deaths by suicide among young professionals was partly due to student loans, either onerous repayments or the fear of default.

Kristine Motlagh, a psychologist who participated in the study and also carries a US$300,000 federal loan commented, 'if you want to have a good life, you get an education. It *has* to be college …'.[13] In other words, if one isn't from a wealthy background then a federal or private loan is the only solution. However, many underestimate the subtle terror this can inflict later on: 'the feeling of hopelessness gets you into a place where you feel like you can't recover'. Repaying the debt anytime soon may seem like an impossible task. A US$100,000 loan with a 6 per cent interest rate requires a US$1100 per month service over a ten-year period. The overall interest paid will be around US$34,500.[14]

The strongest correlation between student debt and suicide ideation seems to peak between US$80 and US$150,000 and then diminishes after that. Presumably, when the amount owed rises above this range, individuals are less worried because repayment is a lost cause. Below this amount the repayments still look doable. Whereas a US$80–150,000 debt is neither dismissible nor doable, this monetary range is the sweet spot when it comes to the psychopathology of modern student finances, the range where credit gets under your skin and takes on sinister existential resonances.

We can understand why some students and graduates thanked their lucky stars when the Covid-19 pandemic hit America hard in 2020. Sure, jobs dried up and campus life ground to a halt. However, many public sector workers had their federal loan repayments paused for six months and the interest rate reduced to 0 per cent.[15] Things are pretty bad when a deadly global pandemic is viewed as a temporary reprieve.

3.

No such relief was provided in the UK though, where student debt has also ballooned. Government figures show outstanding loans at the end of March 2019 topped £121 billion.[16] By 2050 it is predicted that £450 billion (2018–19 prices) will be owed by student debtors. Debt is now so problematic that it can cancel out the 'degree-premium' – the additional income earnt by having a university degree – when young people enter the workforce.[17]

The obvious solution would be to write off this debt, increase public spending and abolish tuition fees. But that option has been completely ignored by government decision-makers. Instead they blame universities for the mess, eliding the fact that higher education providers are simply following the rules set by parliament. The Chairman of the Education Select Committee, for example, lambasted universities for not teaching skills that employers actually want. Only then do student loans become a problem: 'if we are going to continue to lavishly furnish universities with taxpayers' money, we need to think about how universities can specialise in these areas'.[18] The Coronavirus pandemic redoubled this university bashing by state officials, with UK Minister for Universities using the debt crisis to frame his criticisms:

> Too many have been misled by the expansion of popular-sounding courses with no real demand from the labour market. Quite frankly, our young people have been taken advantage of, particularly those without a family history of going to university. Instead some have been left with the debt of an investment that didn't pay off in any sense.[19]

This sentiment epitomises how right-wing critics continue to condemn their own love child, the neoliberal university. According to this narrative, the student loans crisis *isn't* caused by years of state-sponsored commercialisation, slashed public spending or the embarrassing cost of living disaster in England. No, greedy universities are the culprit because they snub proper training and teach classes about Tarabai Shinde instead. Unfortunately, it appears this dubious argument is precisely the one powerful officials are listening to.

Other countries are not faring much better. In New Zealand the nominal value of all loans in 2018 was NZ$15.9 billion, with the overdue student loan debt at NZ$1.3 billion, held mainly by people living overseas.[20] Officials have resorted to arresting defaulters on the border when returning home to visit family. Statistics from Canada and Australia tell a similar story.

The student debt crisis reflects the transition from a Keynesian state apparatus to a neoliberal (or *privatised* Keynesian) system. Total loans have a negative inverse relationship to declining spending as private individuals are forced to absorb the financial burden. What would have once been considered a public investment expenditure (in the pre-1980s period) has been redefined as semi-private debt. The same thing happened with spending reductions across the entire public sector in OECD countries and the tremendous rise of personal credit.[21] Of course, taxation never disappeared. It became regressive instead, offloaded onto individuals in ever devious ways (such as goods and service taxes, charges for access to basic services, etc.), while corporate tax rates dropped to historic lows.

The student loan mess can be traced back to policy changes that semi-privatised tuition overheads as state spending decreased. Each country has its own rendition. The 1997 Dearing report and 2010 Coalition reforms in the UK. The 1992 reauthorisation of the Higher Education Act in the US. The 1994 Todd report in New Zealand. The Dawkins Reforms in Australia during the late 1980s, etc.

But a major ideological sea change had to occur *before* these legislative initiatives could gain support. This began in the US with Human Capital Theory. As mentioned earlier, the concept was devised by scholars at the Chicago School of Economics and originally focused on educational spending.[22] Human Capital sounds rosy and soft on the surface. Cultivate people's skills and talents to make the economy more prosperous. It does contain an unpleasant surprise, however. Who ought to pay for the investment in your human capital? The very phrasing of the question contains the answer, of course. Those who benefit directly in terms of future income ought to cover a growing proportion of investment costs. Echoing the argument made by James B. Buchanan in *Academia in Anarchy*, why should anyone else pay for your fancy science degree?[23]

Of course, the rationale completely omits the extra-individual 'social goods' that everyone enjoys from higher education spending (e.g., more doctors and teachers), an understanding that still holds in Scandinavia, for instance. In the Anglo-American world, however, the discourse of individual ownership has proved difficult to dislodge. Hence why Deutsche Bank recently maintained that student debt remains a 'microproblem' rather than a macro one, an outcome of individual life choices and responsibilities.[24]

The obvious distress endured by those with a debt-sentence has not weakened the resolve of conservative governments. For example, in 2018 then UK prime minster Theresa May said, 'I believe – as do most people, including students – that those who benefit directly from higher education should contribute directly towards the cost of it. That is only fair.'[25] The hypocrisy is typical. Politicians who enjoyed free education 40 years ago are now all in favour of a fees-based system. Another example of the boomer generation pulling the ladder up and debt certainly does have a strong inter-generational component.

This individuation of economic life chances only heightens class divisions in capitalist societies, with tertiary education now a borderline luxury good. Why would a working-class teenager even contemplate entering university if they'll be drowning in loan repayments for the next 30 years? Far better to stack Tesco shelves or flip burgers at McDonalds instead.[26] One must also wonder about the ethics involved here. It seems inexplicable that universities have no moral responsibility for the mass indebtedness they've helped create. The Edu-Factory appears happy to simply take the money and run, letting students cope with the ghastly aftermath alone.

4.

But matters get worse. The neoliberal university is supported by ancillary socio-economic conditions that heap on even more financial difficulties. Just look at the cost of living crises in London, Auckland, Austin and Toronto. Deregulated accommodation markets have fuelled a boom in ultra-expensive yet squalid flats and apartments for students who have little choice but to rent from private landlords. A 2019 study published by the National Union of Students found that 40 per cent of UK students live in flats with mould on their walls.[27] One in five students had insect and rodent infestation problems, including slugs, mice and rats. In London, one of the most expensive cities in the world, additional worries include landlords not returning bonds, poor heating and water supply, unannounced visits from owners and inexplicable rent increases. The subsequent impact on mental health was highlighted in the report. Students were asked about it and their comments included,

> The general worry about the cost of living as a student has a significant toll on students' mental health, including my own.
>
> Knowing that you might not be able to pay rent on time is a constant anxiety. It would affect anyone's mental health.
>
> On Sertraline, an antidepressant, because of stress partly caused by the inability to pay.[28]

These problems taint university-run accommodation as much as those managed privately. One can see why 'rent strikes' have become an effective way of saying 'no'. For example, in 2017 University College London officials partially met striker demands when students withheld their rent for several months.[29] Eviction would look bad so officials decided to concede. Student leaders argued that their members simply couldn't keep up with the payment increases, along with food and other costs, making living in London an almost impossible proposition.

Gender politics intersects with this opportunistic commercial environment. For example, economic desperation is today a major driver of the online 'Sugar Daddy' market, where richer, older men (aka 'Sugar Daddies') connect with young female college students (or 'Sugar Babies') who need help paying rent.[30] Websites like Seekingarrangement.com and Whatsyourprice.com have flourished in this climate, seeing the economic recession as a unique business opportunity. In exchange for financial support, Sugar Babies offer their 'Daddies' a sexual encounter of some description, making it clandestine sex work (but without the 'yuck factor' associated with traditional forms of prostitution).

If we place the abstractions of Human Capital Theory in some all-too-human power relationships, then this is ultimately where it leads. If young women from modest (or even middle-class) backgrounds desire a university degree but cannot afford it and understandably want to avoid crippling levels of debt, this new informal sex industry is waiting. According to Seekingarrangement.com, millions of members have signed up, with a one to four female/male ratio.

Student precarity creates an accessible labour pool for employers who want to keep costs at a bare minimum. This is why during the Coronavirus crisis, many businesses found it remarkably easy to fire workers since they were not properly employed in the first place. But even during ordinary times these job arrangements have raised eyebrows. Take Omar, for instance. He is an international student from Singapore studying in Australia.[31] Omar took a job at a local restaurant to help pay the bills. His employer insisted on a four-hour trial run, which Omar wasn't paid for. His hourly income frequently falls below the minimum national wage.

During his six-hour shift he isn't permitted rest breaks like other workers. Nor does he receive any additional benefits. However, Omar cannot complain since it might jeopardise his job, so he stays quiet instead.

Elsewhere in Australia are other international students like Barack Khan who works at the convenience store 7-Eleven.[32] He describes the role as follows: 'I would call myself a modern century slave where all my rights are gone. I was asked to work sometimes 50 hours, and we had to work ... if we say no, next day we're out of there.' It was alleged that Barack's boss used his visa restrictions (and the threat of deportation) to extract more labour from him. Don't like the poor pay and conditions? Well perhaps we ought to give the Immigration Department a quick call and tell them what you've been up to!

Tensions accompanying the messy conversion of transnational neoliberalism into state corporatism (or 'national neoliberalism') have seen international students experience the university from a stark perspective. For many institutions, the international student market has been a massive money-spinner, raking in billions as the burgeoning middles classes of China and India turn to Western countries to educate their children. Covid-19 nearly bankrupted so many universities because they'd become overreliant on this revenue stream and insouciant about the risks. In any case, countries like Australia allow international students to apply for a temporary student visa, restricting their work rights to 20 hours per week. After entering the workforce they're particularly vulnerable to exploitation. Minimal local knowledge of labour laws and an unwillingness to challenge employers has seen students like Omar and Barack become easy prey to unscrupulous businesses. Their experiences are not isolated cases. A 2017 survey found that 43 per cent of international students in Australia were earning AU$15/hr or less (the minimum wage is AU$18.93/hr).[33]

5.

Let's return to life inside the neoliberal university. It's clearly no pleasure cruise, even if boomers continue to vow that young students have never had it so good. Letters offering 19-year-olds places in the higher education-complex really ought to come with a health warning. After a third Toronto University student died of a suspected suicide in 2019, a protest was launched against the 'toxic campus environment'.[34] The latest death involved an undergrad falling from the Bahen Centre Building to the foyer below. A student rep said he immediately contacted the Vice Provost: 'I mentioned the idea of installing safety nets in the building because we had a similar incident happen earlier this year, they told me they would look into solutions.' But progress was slow. Students were especially angered by how university officials formally announced the tragedies, treating them as isolated incidents and downplaying the obvious pattern. A second-year student remarked, 'the dean's office never specifically mentioned a death or suicide in any emails. I had no idea what was going on, but there was definitely this feeling that something was not right'.[35] With more campus demonstrations planned, the university finally agreed and erected safety barriers in the Bahen Centre Building.

Dark academia affects teachers and students differently, of course. But what I think makes things especially harrowing for students is how they now define their entire self-worth in terms of grade point averages. It isn't difficult to see why. Career prospects in a tight labour market rack up the pressure, especially following the recession caused by the global pandemic. Then there's the crushing parental expectations and the large quantities of money riding on their education. Grades no longer measure academic performance only, but *life performance* as well. What is your score as a human being? All perspective is lost and academic results can take on a life or death urgency. Additional worries about student debt, job insecurity and greedy landlords amplify this false universalisation of academic performance, crowding out other sources of value and dignity. No wonder so many are cracking under the stress. This clearly makes for a very difficult teaching situation too. No one wants to grade students who might interpret the results in such a drastic fashion.

The intense pressure to succeed – coupled with the commoditisation of the educational experience – naturally engenders a very instrumental approach to study. Like many other teachers, I have encountered outlandish examples of 'grade grubbing' in this regard, where students do whatever they can to gain a few extra marks, whether deserved or not. A former grade grubber recalls his rationale for haranguing a professor after receiving a test result:

> I had no real reason to distrust my score on the test. I hadn't even looked at it, for goodness sake, only at the red ink at the top of the first page ... The grade was everything. The grade was the all-important, all-consuming, all-powerful proxy for my identity as a student.[36]

Because students are now cast as consumers who demand success, the power dynamic tilts against the instructor in the classroom: teachers are often (but not always) more willing to compromise standards to produce satisfied customers, with grade inflation a common consequence.[37] Student evaluations and teaching scores exacerbate this unhealthy student/teacher relationship. Research has revealed how filling in a survey at the end of the semester is a poor measure of teaching quality by pedagogical standards.[38] It encourages lecturers to slide into entertainment mode and ease-up when grading essays and exams, whereas teachers who take a more rigorous approach are called boring.[39] In the long run, this hurts students as much as professors because they receive an inferior education.[40] Rating instructors (much like we do Uber drivers) promotes an opportunistic attitude towards learning. Students might pore over the assessment criteria in search for loop holes. Anything for a better result. Acquiring an education – the ultimate purpose of their degree – becomes a secondary objective.

This represents an important transformation: in the neoliberal university students find themselves adopting a weird sort of managerial role, acting as frontline proxies for supervisors in the power hierarchy. The 'boss syndrome' is transmitted down the organisational system as much as up. This accounts for the aggressive disrespect sometimes displayed by students towards teaching staff. It's of little significance that these professionals have trained for years in their respective fields. That's not the point. They exist to serve the customer and can be legitimately hounded with rude emails or targeted on ratemyprofessor.com with tawdry comments about their personal appearance.

6.

Whenever the stakes feel impossibly high, the temptation to cheat is inevitable. The US college admissions scandal involving *Full House* star Lori Loughlin and Felicity Huffman from *Desperate Housewives* demonstrated the lengths some parents will go to beat the system. That scam centred on gaining entry into elite universities. Once inside, however, another world of cheating opportunities presents itself to desperate students. Most institutions use plagiarism detection software like Turnitin or SafeAssign to curb academic misconduct. However, only a cursory glance online reveals hundreds of websites and blogs advising how to hack this software. The rise of 'essay mills' (where students pay someone to write their assignment to spec, also termed 'contract cheating') takes the phenomenon to a new level. Online companies ironically advertise 'plagiarism-free' essays and dissertations, written by experienced scribes who offer bespoke services. And since they're written to order, papers effortlessly slip through anti-plagiarism software. Recent research has found that up to one in seven students around the world have sourced their assignments this way.[41] An essay writer based in China says he charges US$150 per 1000 words and his business turnover can be US$150,000 a year.[42]

One company – EssayShark.com – provides an impressive innovation in this respect, utilising a 'gig economy' business model to match customers and writers, without (potentially incriminating) third-party involvement. The website explains,

> First, our writers check instructions and deadlines of orders, and place their bids in accordance with the complexity and the urgency of particular orders. The system automatically adds a service fee and the total price is displayed to the customer. Then the customer is able to compare all of the bids, as well as get acquainted with each writer's level of cooperation and writing skills by watching him or her start working on the order. This way, a customer can settle for a particular writer whose approach to work and bid requested is most suitable for his or her needs.

The emergence of companies like EssayShark.com is a predictable offshoot of commercialisation. If I've spent tens of thousands on tuition fees and accommodation, then why not a little extra to ease the process? That the university considers essay mills highly illegitimate is irrelevant on one level. This dark market in fraudulent essays is simply the unsavoury flipside of the Edu-Factory. Commodification has always been a double-edged sword in this regard. Think of how organised crime grew exponentially during the heyday of the Washington Consensus. The rampant deregulation of international markets spawned trade in elicit goods and services as much as legal ones.[43]

Anyhow, when I tell my students about how radical the university once was even back in the early 1990s, they look at me with disbelief. Surely the highly financialised and disciplinary machine before them was never like that? Stories about registry sit-ins and spontaneous demonstrations seem unimaginable to them. And I wasn't a professional student activist by any measure! The business-like individualism pervading the university today leaves little mental space for collective dissent. Undergrads are more worried about their next assignment deadline and fees instalment. Compared to that, university politics is a needless distraction. Nevertheless, my argument is this. The student today remains a *radical figure* of sorts, but not in a good way. Debt. Suicide. A pathological focus on grades. Purchasing illegal essays online. An extreme and ruinous unhappiness ... they are following the logic of neoliberalism to its outermost limits.

10

How Universities Die

It's tempting to think that only today does the modern university face a true crisis, particularly with the full ramifications of the 2020 pandemic now beginning to dawn. But even a cursory glance at the historical development of higher education in Western societies indicates that crisis and tumult has never been far away.[1]

Regarding more recent manifestations – following the controversial mass commercialisation of tertiary education as discussed in this book – the 'debate' (if it could be called that) has become polarised: radical calls for a truly free and sheltered university on the one hand (e.g., Jacques Derrida's *L'Université sans condition*) and at the opposite extreme, right-wing manifestos for killing it off once and for all, usually via the market mechanism as libertarian Bryan Caplan suggests.[2] Sadly it seems the latter – 'death-by-market' – provocations coming from Fox News and the Cato Institute are winning the day, in policy terms at least. Here public education especially is in big trouble. At best, the university is considered an auxiliary arm of the knowledge economy and ought to be geared towards producing job-ready graduates. At worst, warped through the anti-intellectual leanings of state populism, public colleges are a total waste of money and need to be radically pared back.

The Covid-19 pandemic, as I have previously suggested, seems to have only bolstered this retrograde twin-attack. The unprecedented global emergency revealed just how money-fixated higher education had become. Tethered to the runaway train of extreme neoliberalism, the modern university is now (institutionally speaking) staring into an abyss: paralysed and unable to turn away from the unforgiving gaze of market realism. Decades of corporatisation have completely derailed higher education's civic mission, unleashing 'academic capitalism' onto the scene; not its laissez-faire variant but one that attracts coercive autocracy, where the fetish of enterprise and big bureaucracy happily coincide. Unlike the entrepreneurial fiction that libertarian economists continue to tout, these institutions attract a great deal of central planning, complete with audit cultures that would make a seasoned accountant blanch. Intellectuality under such conditions is very difficult. Most of the time it is reduced to an arithmetic exercise: counting journal articles, H-index citation scores and grant income totals with little reflection about what 'good' knowledge is, let alone the good life or *eudaimonia*.

If there has been a 'negative dialectic' in the contemporary university following years of economic rationalisation, quietly sublating the norms of academic praxis, then it probably entails a three-step process.[3] First comes the collapse of critical reason into pragmatic utility: hence the prevalence of executive authority and its endless preoccupation with metrics, outputs and income. Ironically, this is often experienced as decidedly impractical by those lower down in the pecking order. Nevertheless, from this managerial perspective if something cannot be measured it doesn't exist. Nay, *should not* exist, since a virulent strain of moralism supplements all those spreadsheets and budgetary forecasts. Indeed, the social dimension isn't eradicated under these conditions, but simply pushed underground.

This brings us to the second dialectical step. It too is negative. Authoritarian quantification inevitably elicits a para-structure of social informality. The rulebook doesn't tell you about this subterranean feature of university life, but off the record it is how things get done. Its lexicon typically consists of deference and amenability, augmenting the functional requirements of the formal power hierarchy. We can call this the *unofficial formal culture* of contemporary higher education.

And that system triggers yet a further flipside, the third and final negation: the shadow within the shadow or the *unofficial informal culture* in academia. Secret backroom deals are made here; careers sabotaged; the worst candidates hired and/or promoted; one may also encounter sexual harassment and bullying. Universities get their reputation for being Machiavellian hotbeds for this reason. Although this underworld is not always congruent with official power – since the freaks and nasties come out to play – it still helps regulate the overarching bureaucratic machine. Outliers implicitly constitute the norm and make it seem reasonable. Here's my key point. All three movements of this dialectical sequence are highly interdependent. In other words, they belong to the same totality. You can see each operating during staff meetings. First are the official pronouncements. Then comes the informal banter that deanlets deploy to soften the blow. And last is the unspoken aggression and frustration lying just beneath the surface. The social dysfunctions created by this final dimension reinforce the official narrative by standing as a scary counterpoint.

Henceforth the personification of academic labour has dramatically evolved. She or he is no longer a collegiate figure of free reason but an overlooked bureaucrat who slaves away writing pointless emails all day. Most desperately want to quit as indicated in the growing (and often hilarious) genre of academic quit lit. But they can't, of course. So *homo academicus* instead cautiously navigates the perils of his or her institution, becoming deft at reading the informal terrain, often to the point of paranoia, sometimes succumbing to gossip and cheap-shot moralising. Some may even try to escape *into* the system, displaying near-psychopathic levels of careerism and overidentifying with journal rankings and grant income to a terrifying degree. In any case, this dialectical triplex permits the impersonal cogs of technocratic rationality to coexist alongside a fickle 'court of judgement', as Adorno and Horkheimer once called it, where public reason is twisted into blind pragmatism and finally dissolves into dark power itself.[4]

But perhaps an even graver turn is afoot. Now that international neoliberalism is turning against itself, a parochial nationalism has flooded higher education, even in the great global cities of London, New York and Montreal. Universal logos, once the vanguard of the enlightenment project is now (again) in tatters as it descends into *Deliverance*-style localism. Universities can no longer even glean the cosmopolitan crumbs that dropped from the table of globalisation and the Washington Consensus. You see this in HR departments and their regulation of expat employees. Tertiary education providers today function as surrogate border control agents – something that HR seems pleased to do, by the way – ensuring staff have their papers in order.

In the wake of Brexit and the Mexico Wall, universities in England and the US have enforced this 'paper checking' *reductio ad absurdum*. Between 2016 and 2018 the number of F-1 student visas issued in the US dropped by 22 per cent.[5] The Covid-19 crisis gave the US government further license to propose backward policies, threatening to withdraw F-1 and M-1 visas for international students whose courses had gone online.[6] In the UK, academics are regularly threatened with deportation and their loved ones refused residency. Institutions monitor 'right to work' documentation with grim determination, even when academics generously offer their time for doctoral examinations at other institutions or sit on exam boards. Show us your work permit!

As a New Zealander, my 15 years in the UK system drove me nuts for this reason. The underlying message wasn't difficult to decipher: foreigners are no longer welcome. In the US, Canada and Australasia too, the international recruitment of academics appears to be declining, even in universities that rely on the global student market for economic survival. None of this bodes well. Unpredictable events like Coronavirus only surface the menacing trends that were already well advanced anyway.

The symptoms of terminal decline are not just economic, however. Institutions that still enjoy surpluses are also dying inside, overcome by a mood of mute desperation and melancholia. With their public mission in disarray and teachers little more than knowledge-based production-line operators, morale has reached an all-time low. The trouble is that the cause of this occupational malaise – the businessification of higher education – is still being pushed as the cure. Almost every government report on universities in the Western world continues to recommend the same old thing: more impact; more corporate management; more performance-based incentives; more deregulation of tuition fees; more market competition. More ... more ... more ...

The seriously ill patient before us displays tell-tale signs that their life support system is in major trouble. Let's examine some of the more apparent symptoms.

- **Symptom 1**: Private universities tend to be less corporate than public ones since they have nothing to prove.

Ushered in over the last decade or two, an oversupply of commercial simulacra – the institutional mimicking of the corporate world as it is *imagined* to be in its purist form – is a defining feature of the neoliberal university, particularly in countries that have eviscerated their wider public sphere. The simulation process is always only limited, of course. On the one hand, marketisation and management hierarchies certainly conform to a certain spirit of the private enterprise. On the other, however, a doctrine of strict austerity prevails, even when surpluses are bountiful. Staff don't partake in the same benefits that big business employees enjoy. Barring a few elite institutions, there are no corporate credit cards, generous bonuses, tax write-offs, personal secretaries, guaranteed parking or business class flights in academia, accept for those at the apex of the university, of course.

As I argued earlier, this emulation of corporations by publicly funded universities would seem like an oxymoron if it wasn't for the discourse of New Public Management. This was imposed by successive governments and their army of vapid 25-year-old consultants. Fiscal accountability, with its emphasis on targets, cost efficiency and thrift, is applauded not in the name of 'the corporation' but value for money and taxpayers' dollars well spent. This is why the contemporary university can praise the virtues of public education and still exude an archetypal capitalist ethos. Isn't it ironic? After coming out the other end, the public university may be more corporate than the corporation itself, but tells itself the exact opposite (for example, universities in the UK are technically 'charities').

In any case, given the staggering amounts of government money flowing into the corporate sector (through direct/indirect subsidies, tax breaks and quantitative easing after the financial crisis), one has to wonder why big business doesn't have to abide by the same strict standards of accountability as universities, hospitals and public broadcasters. Perhaps it's because the for-profit corporation is so adored by the power elite that they are still trusted to regulate themselves no matter how much they fail in this respect. Whereas public universities are viewed with malign suspicion. Hence our first symptom as it pertains to the dying university. Most private (nonprofit) colleges, big or small, don't have to deal with this schizophrenic public/private antinomy and thus avoid the worst convulsions as neoliberalism crashes and burns.

- **Symptom 2**: The rapid growth of administrative personnel in universities hardly ever relieves academics of administrative labour, but the exact opposite, almost always to the detriment of overall productivity.

To simplify things somewhat, there are good bureaucracies and bad ones.[7] Good bureaucracies are socially enabling and creative, linked to common governance goals, with power being held in check by the lowest common denominator. The bad ones tend to be hermetic disciplinary systems, with the apex remote from everyone else, including citizens, workers and customers. Unfortunately, it's the latter type that have burgeoned in the corporate university.

Bureaucracy has always had self-replicating qualities, where rules and administrative personnel seem to increase of their own accord. Back in the 1950s, sociologists like Alvin Gouldner and Peter Blau noticed this in large enterprises and recorded the strange behaviour it caused.[8] For example, managers will often seek to legitimate their own roles within the institution above all else. *Bureaucratic ritualisation* is where meetings are held for the sake of meetings and considered an 'output' rather than an input towards other objectives. Similarly, *goal displacement* occurs when red-tape becomes an end in itself. Paperwork escalates to the point where it begins to undermine organisational effectiveness and morale, often triggering *more* bureaucracy to deal with the subsequent dysfunctions.

These glitches are manifest in universities too. The main problem with the growth of non-teaching/non-research managers is this: they're infamous for creating a huge amount of subsidiary work or 'white noise' in an organisational ecology, much of which is worthless but simply cannot be ignored. This is tantamount to box-ticking and hoop jumping labour rather than value-adding work like teaching, research and programme coordinating. Hence why overwork *and* under-productivity can weirdly coincide in admin-heavy institutions. It's not uncommon to find university departments with relatively modest outputs yet have an exhausted and stressed workforce for this very reason.

- **Symptom 3**: The Covid-19 pandemic confirmed what we suspected all along: information technology, especially email, is the enemy of academic freedom.

Email has become the medium *and* the message of office work in the post-industrial economy. It has systematically and surreptitiously lengthened the working day and narrowed communication to a set of command-words, with little nuance or depth. BlackBerry mobile phones, for example, were first designed for managers to send subordinates telegraphic directives. Given the ease and psychological distance it affords, office email has taken on a life of its own, becoming something of a minor tyranny in academia.[9]

When first-generation email was adopted by IBM in the early 1980s, it was intended to help employees transfer files within the company. However, the server soon crashed.[10] The amount of traffic overwhelmed the network because people began to use it for *all* communication. Digital mainframes are much improved today, but the same flaw applies. The sheer amount of emails that ordinary academics receive on a daily basis is ridiculous. If we were to sit down and answer them from 8am onwards, especially on Monday mornings, by the time the first batch was done, replies to earlier messages would soon be piling up, requiring renewed attention. This feeling of ad infinitum characterises the phenom-enological angst of office email more generally.

Furthermore, in the Edu-Factory *speed* (or at least the percep-tion of it) is everything, especially concerning student feedback. I remember chairing a two-hour meeting one morning. After-wards I received a phone call from my programme officer. A grad student was asking why I hadn't replied to his email. I confessed the last few days had been pretty busy – I probably missed it in the deluge. After looking for the student's message I discovered it had actually been sent during the meeting an hour ago. Because an immediate reply had not been sent, they complained. I swiftly deleted the email before walking to the next meeting.

The global Coronavirus pandemic and campus closures revealed the true nature of information communication technolo-gies in academia. After the labour process was moved online it was painful to read newspaper columns like, 'What Films Should You Watch in Lockdown?' and 'Pandemic Blues: Boredom and Daytime TV'. University workloads peaked during the crisis, making late-night TV a luxury let alone its daytime variant. An expectation was set early on. Working online meant academics were pretty much *always* on-call, available to undertake tasks and supply information within a moment's notice. If email was an inconspicuous taskmaster before Covid-19, it was now proudly stepping centre-stage and calling the shots. Here work and life truly did blur, as 'biopolitical' theories of late capitalism predicted, with misbehaving children and barking dogs inadvertently partic-ipating in Zoom meetings too. With academics sitting glued to their laptops for interminable periods, one can only imagine the amount of unpaid overtime they expended.

The trouble with email is that it follows the classic time/effort bell curve. In the beginning productivity increases. But after a certain point the time spent on email starts to hinder productivity, intelligence and awareness. Researchers once did an experiment comparing an email-immersed workplace with one in which the *same* job was conducted without email access.[11] Overall productivity during the day was dramatically improved in the email-free office. Productivity isn't the real issue here, however. My gripe with email is the sheer inanity of the messages one is forced to read and write. As a mode of social interaction it both dulls the senses and incites unnecessary anxiety.

- **Symptom 4**: Universities struggling in national/global league tables are often more aggressive and unrealistic about the idea of joining the elite few, damaging staff goodwill in the process and thus reinforcing their reputation as a substandard institution.

National and international university league tables are part of the new ranking mania that's swept higher education over the last 20 years. Before this, we had a rough idea of who the so-called 'top' universities were, informed mainly by historical prestige (Oxbridge, the Ivy League, etc.) and renowned research. That system was often inaccurate and unfair, of course. So when these tables first appeared – numerically 'stack-ranking' all universities in a country or even globally – it was said they would provide a more transparent picture of quality. And in the age of market choice and fiscal accountability, this was deemed essential. It also helped keep universities on their toes and eschew complacency, something that government funders were very keen on.

Who designs these tables? It's isn't just government agencies, but newspapers (the *Financial Times* and *Guardian*, for example) and various non-academic organisations too. And similar to the accreditation assurance bodies that have also accrued considerable clout, these ranking authorities (like Ranking Web of Universities) have wedged themselves between students and the university, using middleman tactics to build their own brand power. Anyway, one cannot find a university today in the UK, Europe, North America and Australasia that doesn't profess an ambition to be in the top percentile of whatever league table they're obsessed with. The problem is obvious. Given the sheer number of universities, not all can be in the 'Russell Group' or 'Top 10'. So rather than abandon this unrealistic ambition and do something creative instead, senior managers chase it even more ardently. The expectation is then lumped onto staff with increasingly punitive performance measures. As a result, these universities often become horrible places to work. Word of mouth spreads in academic circles, deterring good researchers (and often students) from going anywhere near them. And as new league tables are published, the cycle begins again.

- **Symptom 5**: As an individual advances up the university management hierarchy, the more they will assert the importance of teaching, which is inversely proportional to the amount of teaching they actually do.

Teaching is a core university activity and most academics seek to excel at this difficult task. Difficult because (for most of us, at least) teaching doesn't come naturally and requires a good deal of preparation, effort and practice to get right. Both students and teachers are greatly rewarded when this happens. However, the corporate university changes this pedagogical moment in three ways. First, class size is crucial for generating maximum revenue, resulting in the massification of student numbers. Second, tuition fees transform students into fickle customers, significantly altering their expectations in the process. And third, students quantitatively score teaching performance, with the results linked to career progression and rewards.

In non-elite institutions at least, teaching becomes both a stressful experience (for staff and students alike), yet vital to the financial sustainability of the university. Academics recruited to management often avoid teaching like the plague – not because they're too busy, but because they know how rebarbative it can be under neoliberal conditions. Given their 'helicopter view' of the institution's economic status, senior managers will nevertheless extol the virtues of teaching. For those in the trenches, delivering classes with 700 students, the scenario is made worse if their Associate Dean of Learning Excellence neither teaches nor is required to grade 400 exam scripts within a four-day deadline.

- **Symptom 6**: The more emphasis placed on 'student satisfaction', the less substantial their education will be.

This symptom of decline seems counterintuitive until it is examined within the commercialised conditions of higher education today. What does learning really mean? As opposed to what Paulo Freire called the 'banking method' of education (where teachers deposit prepackaged info-bits into a passive receptacle), critical pedagogy urges the *reciprocal agency* of both teacher and student, leading to the acquisition of tacit (rather than just formal) skill and reflexivity.[12] This often involves a struggle. Received wisdom is internally confronted and scrutinised, encouraging independent thinking and judgement. Students are always at the centre of the process, but never as an entertained audience who are spoon-fed Power-Point slides. Delayed gratification is crucial to proper learning.[13]

This mode of education is nearly impossible to deliver when class sizes are huge. Oftentimes students may not even attend lectures if the material is available online. Moreover, the customer-centric discourse structurally encourages them to focus on the means (essay grades and marks) as an end in itself. This changes the entire learning culture. For example, one could argue that a student who receives 50 per cent for an essay may have had a superior learning experience given the feedback received. Next time they will do better. All educationalists understand that error is an indispensable feature of long-term knowledge acquisition. But today the student will immediately assume they've had an inferior experience and score the lecturer accordingly.

Nor is the ensuing 'personality contest' only something lecturers must grapple with in the brave new classroom. Students too often play this wrongheaded game on *themselves*. They mistake grades as markers for their overall intelligence, which then signals whether they're a good person or not. Now that academic careers and rewards are tagged to teaching scores, instructors will inevitably adjust their approach, opting for satisfied customers instead of educated citizens.

• **Symptom 7**: Over time academic metrics end up measuring only one thing. The extent of their own reification.

The fetishisation of academic metrics is a central characteristic of the contemporary university and a powerful incentive system across the disciplines. Journal ranking lists in particular have changed how academic labour is coordinated and evaluated by peers and managers. As we have seen, when the measure becomes the target then leading journals obtain inordinate power. But the ranking process is very self-referential. So-called 'top' journals are seldom neutral barometers of quality. They have implicit biases (regarding format, topics, methodologies, etc.) that authors must accept in order to be considered for publication. This is in turn linked to informal networks that operate behind the scenes. Ranking quants mention none of this, of course. As Royal Holloway professor, Chris Grey, notes,

> there is a circularity, in which to publish in the 'best' journals, one must produce the 'right kind' of work. Ambitious scholars who aspire to be the best tend to learn to conform to this kind of work. The 'best' journals therefore publish the work of the 'best' scholars and are able to reproduce themselves as the elite for this reason.[14]

That single-authored articles in top-tier journals ever became the gold standard for gauging academic excellence, it must be remembered, was the product of a historical struggle that academics lost. The depressing part about this symptom is the continuing complicity of the vanquished. Some scholars aim to publish in leading journals *before* they've written a paper, sometimes *before* they even have a topic. It is now difficult to even remember what it was like before journal rankings, so entrenched are they. It's like trying to imagining office life before email.

- **Symptom 8**: The more prominent work-life balance and mental wellbeing programmes are in a university, the greater licence they will have to condone chronic overwork.

Usually emanating from HR, platitudes concerning work-life balance are common in the neoliberal university. According to the official line, employers have a duty of care to help employees develop healthy work habits. Managers must remind staff to take annual leave, utilise fitness centres, avoid email during unsociable hours and complete online tutorials about mental wellbeing in the workplace. Meditation and yoga classes are sometimes even offered to accentuate the point.

Universities don't do all this out of kindness. There is a strong business case for work-life balance programmes since the economic costs of burnout can be significant. More importantly, universities are protected from compensation claims that stem from overwork if they have previously offered advice about work-life balance. In this context, the Edu-Factory's assembly-line may actually be *sped up* when such programmes are present. Sure, there are a zillion tasks to complete within a fixed timeframe and we do implicitly expect you to work beyond contracted hours, including weekends and nights. But if you're stressed and hurting then the ball's in your court since you did successfully complete that mandatory 'Healthy Workplaces Are Happy Workplaces' training module.

The mixed message isn't part of some masterplan but more the outcome of over-administration and detached power hierarchies.

Recall the automated workload allocation email that Cardiff University staff received on Saturday morning following the suicide of Malcom Anderson (discussed in Chapter 6). It's tempting to infer rational planning here, imagining some senior administrator devising ever more sinister methods for cracking the whip. But it is probably more likely that an *absence* of thinking was the driving factor, radical non-thought.[15] At any rate, work-life balance programmes mainly seek to minimise employer liability, with most executive managers happy to avert their eyes from the main reason why exhaustion is endemic in higher education today.

- **Symptom 9**: Neoliberal universities present a fairly complete microcosm of the 'white male' privilege dominating Western society as a whole, irrespective of their lush equality and diversity policies.

The figures speak for themselves. In the US, this is the demographic distribution of full-time professors: 54 per cent white males, 27 per cent white females, 8 per cent Asian/pacific islander males and 3 per cent Asian/pacific islander females. Only 2 per cent of full-time professors are black males, black females or Hispanic males.[16] If we look at the racial structure of the student body in the US, 61 per cent are white, 18 per cent Hispanic, 12.3 per cent black, 5.7 per cent Asian and 0.7 per cent American Indian.[17] Colleges in the US tend to be spaces of whiteness and reflect little of the diversity that's often depicted in marketing campaigns. Yet the alt-right still disparages universities for being strongholds of multiculturalism, political correctness and male-hating militants. Enrolment and employment statistics, however, indicate otherwise.

Upon entering the neoliberal university, these racial and gender dynamics can make life hell for those who don't fit the white male profile. A 2019 survey of UK universities discovered around one quarter of students from an ethnic minority background have experienced racial harassment.[18] 56 per cent (of this proportion) have been subjected to racist name-calling, insults and jokes. Staff weren't immune either. 50 per cent of those surveyed said they'd been ignored or excluded because of their race and one quarter had racist slurs or jokes targeted at them. So much for the postmodern Marxism that Donald Trump Jr and Jordan Peterson adamantly insist has infiltrated university campuses.

- **Symptom 10**: No matter how grim it gets working in the contemporary university, the general public will presume otherwise. For them, campus life exudes an aura of exemption and mystique. By default, academics who criticise the corporate university are perceived to be somehow self-serving and ungrateful.

I remember bumping into a next door neighbour after weeks of heavy teaching. 'I haven't seen you in ages,' she said, 'been buried in the books?' My neighbour knew I was an academic and assumed I'd been closeted away in the library studying. The truth was I hadn't read a book in months. My time was instead consumed with teaching, marking, managing programmes and dealing with the associated administrative sludge. When free time was available, I felt drained and listened to Elliott Smith instead.

The depiction of university life expressed by my neighbour is reminiscent of C.P Snow's *The Masters* or Robin Williams' character in *Good Will Hunting*. It is incredibly inaccurate and outdated, yet frustratingly persistent for some reason. There is no recondite club of tweed-jacketed, pipe smoking professors who think all day and pen esoteric research papers once every few years. Nevertheless, this fairytale about the profession – of Cambridge dons standing before the high table reciting Latin prayers – has been exceptionally handy for transforming the modern university into a formidable industrial-complex. Academics have nothing to moan about! Living the life of Riley I tell you!

I realise one must not get too carried away with this line of argument. Compared to a large electronics factory in Shenzhen, China, the corporate university is still a walk among the tulips. But it certainly isn't the idyllic sanctuary of study that so many still assume. As for reading books – let alone writing them – they remain low on the priority list ... very low indeed. Apart from global pandemics, bad management and hostile government budgets, perhaps this is really how universities die.

Conclusion
Are Some Lost Causes Truly Lost?

Early in my career, shortly after arriving in England, I was shocked when an academic in my field committed suicide. I had only met her a few times, but friends knew her well. The 45-year-old professor had suffered bouts of depression after a divorce. When she hanged herself at home, the university paid its condolences and celebrated her as a wonderful researcher, teacher and colleague. Later on a more troubled version of events emerged. The London professor – a leading expert on workplace bullying and stress – had taken on a major service role in her university. By all accounts, the workload was challenging. The coroners' inquest concluded that she was under 'huge stress', particularly concerning the technology.[1] A senior university spokesman later admitted that before committing suicide, 'a number of matters about getting things done with the job' had been raised by the academic.[2]

I remember putting this tragedy aside as an awful aberration, a one-off incident that certainly wasn't representative of the occupation as a whole. This view has slowly changed over the years, which subsequently became a motivation for writing this book.

I was reflecting on this sad memory while revising an early draft and then the Covid-19 pandemic struck. It was an unprecedented event in higher education. All bets were off. Jobs were on the line. But here's my point. The bureaucratic economism that has gradually colonised the university over the previous two decades was suddenly in full view during the crisis, warts and all. The grinder and its superintendents were stripped of those familiar bromides regarding collegiality and civic purpose: ultimately, the university is a business enterprise and don't get any funny ideas otherwise. Even unions couldn't come up with a counter-narrative to oppose this financialised outlook as redundancies loomed. That's how hegemony works. Economic exceptionalism (typically with reference to 'sustainability') marginalises political questions about how the university ought to be run and its ultimate social mission. The pandemic did not pause or displace the latent dysfunctions that foreshadowed the above suicide. On the contrary, it has crystallised them into a sharper form.

What is the purpose of a university? To create important new fields of understanding and extend existing knowledge-bases, whether in terms of applied expertise, empirical examination and/or conceptual insights.[3] This ought to better humankind on multiple levels, including the physical, theoretical, political, cultural, environmental and economic dimensions of life. In the final instance, the university serves to cultivate and democratise reason and the global benefits it can yield.

Under what institutional conditions should these objectives be pursued? Over the last 35 years, government officials, university councillors and senior managers have answered, 'through the market'. More fee-paying students. Bigger external grants. Private endowments. Performance-based management systems that attract and incentivise staff and so forth. As I've argued in previous chapters, this may look innocuous on paper, from a notional standpoint. But in the trenches, even for established professors as the opening example indicates, the pressures have become intense and counterproductive. The ideology of free market education assumes a profound *materialist* aspect, in which the human body itself becomes the topography of the maladaptations that can transpire.

Staff are obviously unhappy with this brave new world of higher education and have resorted to various coping mechanisms. Some see the writing on the wall and decide to embrace academic capitalism. That's always disappointing to witness. Others opt for a sort of schizophrenic existence, displaying the trappings of corporate academia while inwardly adhering to the 'old values'. The end result is often a vague feeling of absurdity. Another response is to hide and hope to be left alone. In an era of high technocracy, however, that's increasingly difficult. Early retirement provides an exit route for over 50s, but what about everyone else? Building stronger unions is clearly an important way forward

– collectively countering the dominant norms and calling them out as outrageous. Yet most unions appear ineffective when truly put to the test by open acts of intimidation, as the 2018–20 UK pensions dispute revealed. And one wonders how they will oppose the job cuts following the global Coronavirus pandemic.

We are left with the same problem this book began with. The commoditisation of universities (along with the managerialism and cut-throat work cultures it encourages) runs deep today, almost to the bottom. So here we should return to the classic Kantian question about whether hope is justified. Can the university be saved? It is difficult to answer this question without nostalgically longing for some golden past. But let's face it: universities were never pristine domains of liberty before New Public Management and market discipline took over (although I do smile when remembering how 25 years ago professors still smoked in their offices and kept an obligatory bottle of Johnny Walker Red in the filing cabinet).

If hope is to be redeemed, it must be placed within the constraints of the present juncture, which is bleak and wreckage-like. Moreover, seeing future possibilities in the present allows us to better survey the damage in a sober light and hopefully chart a path out. As Herbert Marcuse put it (in a different but not entirely unrelated context), 'the destructiveness of the present stage reveals its full significance only if the present is measured, not in terms of past stages, but in terms of its own potentialities'.[4]

With respect to the contemporary university, two fascinating ethico-political strategies have appeared that are worth considering.

The first is the idea of a *university without condition* (or limits imposed by the marketplace, money, government enmity, etc.) that Jacques Derrida proposed a few years before his death.[5] This model of higher education enjoys full dispensation from state and market capitalism, with a 'no strings attached' funding structure included. The university without condition thus feels extremely remote, even utopian compared to the current situation ... but in a good way: 'this university demands and ought to be granted in principle, besides what is called academic freedom, an unconditional freedom to question and to assert, or even, going still further, the right to say publicly all that is required by research, knowledge, and thought concerning the truth'.[6]

Remember that Derrida's universitas is an 'ideal-type' and he is trying to distil its abstract potential into pure principles, *in potentia* rather than *in actu*. That is why, 'this university without conditions does not, in fact, exist, as we know only too well. Nevertheless, in principle and in conformity to its declared vocation, its professed essence, it should remain an ultimate place of critical resistance – and more than critical – to all the powers of dogmatic and unjust appropriation.'[7] We can see this idea echoed by liberal critics of the neoliberal university too, like Stefan Collini, who plea for a protected space, immunity from university bashing politicians and their mean-spirited funding policies.[8]

The second approach is different. It recognises how the 'university without condition' tarries with an insurmountable impasse or *aporia* that will be very difficult to overcome (it is Derrida after all!). This isn't ideal for practical resistance, especially in a post-Covid-19 context as governments prime public universities for a formidable 'market correction'. Stefano Harney and Fred Moten thus posit a more fugitive stratagem for studying and working in higher education today.[9] Their inspiration comes not from any utopian ideal but the scattered vagabonds who *already* wander the darklands of the undercommons; the overlooked majority who labour within, against and under the university but remain frustratingly unvalorised, particularly when its collective efforts are so essential as is the case today.

What is exactly 'under' when it comes to this commons? The concept refers to the invisible cooperation that occurs beneath the ossified structures of official authority, within the burnt-out basement of the edifice. This was once called collegiality, but is much more than that now given how collegiality has been effectively hijacked by a sort of hyper-professionalism. The point is, knowledge itself has become the means of production, and that cannot be separated from the social cooperation and living labour of academics themselves, which remains independent to executive power, although clearly controlled by it.[10]

The university secretly depends on the undercommons to operate yet cannot (formally, at least) muster this social energy using the technocratic methods it only knows. Think here of the immense informal labour undertaken by faculty and their families during the Covid-19 crisis, in which senior management was often an onlooker when teaching was moved online. Most importantly, this labour is not a 'resource' as HR might define it because it gains its very form and vitality by resisting that category, refusing its own objectification. While so evidently reliant on this unpaid work, the corporate university must nevertheless dismiss and malign it. Why so? Because it would reveal that management hierarchies and their factory-like incentive systems are largely superfluous and obstructive to the academic labour process, including teaching and research:

even as [the modern university] depends on these moles, these refugees, it will call them uncollegial, impractical, naive, unprofessional. And one may be given one last chance to be pragmatic – why steal when one can have it all, they will ask. But if one hides from this interpellation, neither agrees nor disagrees but goes with hands full into the underground of the university, into the Undercommons – this will be regarded as theft, as a criminal act. And it is at the same time, the only possible act.[11]

However, the undercommon is riven by a decisive 'general antagonism'. Politically and organisationally speaking, it cannot fully be what it already is.

So on the one hand we have a political ethics galvanised by the *future anterior* (that may never arrive) and on the other a *fugitive clandestiny* (that's forever fleeing bureaucratic incorporation but can never quite do so). Alone each are not enough, of course. Mention Derrida's 'university without condition' at your next faculty meeting and see how far you get. As for the undercommons, it could easily remain that: an underground bolthole that makes little difference to the prevailing architecture of power.[12]

But imagine if we could discern a point of convergence between these two modes of refusal, wouldn't that be truly emancipatory?

I'm unsure if it can be done. But a number of speculative resonances can be detected. For starters, both Derrida's forlorn optimist and Harney and Moten's shapeshifting fugitive find it *impossible* to go on like this, to continue living as such under the dominion of academic capitalism. The time for compromise and adapting to reality is over. We might call this an 'anti-Beckettian' turn in politics.[13] In part, the realisation takes its cue from how the social body has been pushed to its limits in the Edu-Factory. Our collective physiology is flagging in front of us as hypertension and exhaustion set in. But it also emanates from the sense of having been abandoned by our calling. This transfigures the political contradictions of academic capitalism into an existential inflection point or *krisis*: is this really how we want to spend the irreplaceable time that remains? In any case, to remain a scholar who is faithful to the vocation today is impossible unless something gives.

Apart from quitting academia (perhaps to become a truck driver), this *krisis* can basically lead in two directions. Either the impossibility is transcended through the objective negation of the reality-principle and its radical repossession so we might live again (e.g., reclaiming the means of academic production, etc.). Or the negation is turned inwards towards the self and its annihilation, the tragic path taken by the academic described earlier. If the latter option is untenable, then isn't the former wild and wishful thinking in terms of transformative change?

Yes, probably.

In reprising the Kantian question of whether hope is permissible, one that is intimately linked not just to the prospect of happiness but more importantly, 'the worthiness to be happy', I remain pessimistic.[14] The corporate university is essentially a *symptom* of powerful constellations lying beyond its own remit. Managers, scholars and students still have agency, of course. But the institutional field is overdetermined and formidably delimited by the state first, the market and economic matrix second and the corporate industrial-complex third, which increasingly define the macro-rules of the game we must play. As it circles the drain, this tripartite has gripped society even more decisively – including higher education – and now threatens to drag us down with it into a dark new beginning.

Notes

Websites last accessed 31 July 2020.

INTRODUCTION

1. Walsh, J. (2020). 'The Coming Disruption: Scott Galloway predicts a handful of elite cyborg universities will soon monopolize higher education.' *New York Magazine*. Available at https://nymag.com/intelligencer/2020/05/scott-galloway-future-of-college.html
2. For example, see Boyd, R. (2020). 'Zoom and Gloom: Universities in the Age of COVID-19'. *Los Angeles Review of Books*. Available at https://lareviewofbooks.org/article/zoom-and-gloom-universities-in-the-age-of-covid-19/. For a related analysis, see Kunkler, B. (2020). 'Australian Universities Were Sick Before the Pandemic'. *Jacobin Magazine*. Available at https://jacobinmag.com/2020/04/australian-universities-coronavirus-austerity-funding-privatization
3. Smyth, J. (2018). *The Toxic University: Zombie Leadership, Academic Rock Stars and Neoliberal Ideology*. London: Palgrave Macmillan; Newfield, C. (2018). *The Great Mistake: How We Wrecked Public Universities and How We Can Fix Them*. Baltimore: Johns Hopkins University Press; Labaree, D. (2017). *A Perfect Mess: The Unlikely Ascendancy of American Higher Education*. Chicago: University of Chicago Press; Readings, B. (1996). *The University in Ruins*. Cambridge, MA: Harvard University Press; Schrecker, E. (2010). *The Lost Soul of Higher Education: Corporatization, the Assault on Academic Freedom and the End of the America University*. New York: New Press; Cottom, T.M. (2016). *Lower Ed: The Troubling Rise of For-Profit Colleges in the New Economy*. New York: New Press; Hill, R. (2012). *Whackademia: An Insider's Account of the Troubled University*. Sydney: University of New South Wales Press.
4. Kezar, A. and DePaola, T. (2019). *The Gig Academy: Mapping Labor in the Neoliberal University*. Baltimore: Johns Hopkins University Press. Also see Chakrabortty, A. and Weale, S. (2016). 'Universities Accused of "Importing Sports Direct model" for Lecturers'

Pay'. *Guardian*. Available at www.theguardian.com/uk-news/2016/nov/16/universities-accused-of-importing-sports-direct-model-for-lecturers-pay

CHAPTER 1

1. Hainey, F. (2018). 'Coventry University Accused of "Dirty Tricks" by Trade Union Fighting for Recognition'. *Coventry Telegraph*. Available at www.coventrytelegraph.net/news/coventry-news/coventry-university-accused-dirty-tricks-14468380

2. Erickson, M., Hanna, P. and Walker, C. (2020). 'The UK Higher Education Senior Management Survey: A Statactivist Response to Managerialist Governance'. *Studies in Higher Education*. doi: 10.1080/03075079.2020.1712693

3. Commentators have been drawing an analogy between industrial production methods and the modern university for some time. In his famous 1917 lecture 'The Scholar's Work' (often translated as 'Science as a Vocation') Max Weber describes the decline of the Humboldtian principle of *universitas litterarum*. Weber argued that the Americanisation of German institutions had induced factory-like conditions between senior university officials and instructors: 'we encounter the condition that is found wherever capitalist enterprise comes into operation: the "separation of the worker from his means of production". The worker, that is, the assistant, is dependent upon the implements that the state puts at his disposal; hence he is just as dependent on the head of the institute as is the employee in a factory upon the management ... the assistant's position is often as precarious as is that of any "quasi-proletarian" existence ...' (p. 131). The analogy was more recently used by Stanley Aronowitz in his excellent and far-reaching critique of the neoliberal university, *The Knowledge Factory*. And finally, the terminology itself derives from an activist organisation of the same name. See Weber, M. (1917/1946). 'Science as a Vocation'. In *From Max Weber: Essays in Sociology*, Trans. H.H. Girth and C. Wright Mills. New York: Oxford University Press, pp. 129–56; Aronowitz, S. (2000). *The Knowledge Factory: Dismantling the Corporate University and Creating True Higher Learning*. Boston, MA: Beacon Press. See Edu-Factory Collective (2009). *Towards a Global Autonomous University*. New York: Autonomedia.

4. Hall, R. and Batty, D. (2019). 'Students Protest Against Liverpool University's Claim That Support for Strike Is "Unlawful"'. *Guardian*. Available at www.theguardian.com/education/2019/nov/29/students-protest-against-liverpool-universitys-claim-that-support-for-strike-is-unlawful

5. Segran, E. (2014). 'The Adjunct Revolt: How Poor Professors Are Fighting Back'. *The Atlantic*. Available at www.theatlantic.com/business/archive/2014/04/the-adjunct-professor-crisis/361336/

6. Ryan, S. (2012). 'Academic Zombies: A Failure of Resistance or a Means of Survival'. *Australian Universities Review*. 54(2): 3–11.

7. Lesnick-Oberstein, K.E. et al. (126 signatories) (2015). 'Let UK Universities Do What They Do Best – Teaching and Research'. *Guardian*. Available at www.theguardian.com/education/2015/jul/06/let-uk-universities-do-what-they-do-best-teaching-and-research?

8. Berg, M. and Seeber, B. (2017). *The Slow Professor: Challenging the Culture of Speed in the Academy*. Toronto: Toronto University Press; Gannon, K.M. (2020). *Radical Hope: A Teaching Manifesto*. Morgantown: West Virginia University Press; Connell, R. (2019). *The Good University: What Universities Actually Do and Why It's Time for Change*. Melbourne: Monash University Press. We might also add Fitzpatrick, K. (2019). *Generous Thinking: A Radical Approach to Save the University*. Baltimore: Johns Hopkins University Press; Noble, M. and Ross, C. (eds) (2019). *Reclaiming the University for the Public Good: Experiments and Futures in Co-operative Higher Education*. London: Palgrave Macmillan.

9. 'What may I hope?', asks Kant in his most famous critique. See Kant, I. (1781/1998). *Critique of Pure Reason*, Trans. Paul Guyer and Allen W. Wood. Cambridge: Cambridge University Press, p. 677.

10. Respectively, see Lukianoff, G. and Haidt, J. (2018). *The Coddling of the American Mind: How Good Intentions and Bad Ideas Are Setting up a Generation for Failure*. New York: Penguin; Caplan, B. (2018). *The Case Against Education: Why the Education System Is a Waste of Time and Money*. Princeton: Princeton University Press; Shapiro, B. (2004). *Brainwashed: How Universities Indoctrinate America's Youth*. Nashville: WMD Books.

11. For Caplan, higher education is nothing more than social signalling and a waste of time when it comes to useful job skills. See Caplan, B. (2020). 'COVID on Campus (with Bryan Caplan)'. *Libertarian*.

org. Available at www.libertarianism.org/podcasts/building-tomor-row/covid-campus-bryan-caplan

12. A recent example comes from the US Secretary of Education, Betsy DeVos. In 2019 she pushed hard for reforms that would relax accreditation requirements for private higher education providers: 'we ended the stranglehold that a system designed when people travelled by horse and buggy continued to have on institutions', DeVos stated as the legislation was being finalised. That predatory and corrupt opportunists subsequently entered the sector is not surprising. A recent report found that one 'Reagan National University' had no students or faculty, yet was fully accredited under the new initiative. US Department of Education. (2019). 'Secretary DeVos Finalizes Higher Education Regulations That Promote Innovation, Protect Students, and Reduce Regulatory Burden'. Available at www.ed.gov/news/press-releases/secretary-devos-finalizes-higher-education-regulations-promote-innovation-protect-students-and-reduce-regulatory-burden; Quintana, C. and Conlon, S. (2020). 'This College Was Accredited by a DeVos-Sanctioned Group. We Couldn't Find Evidence of Students or Faculty.' *USA Today.* Available at www.usatoday.com/story/news/education/2020/02/15/college-accreditation-department-education-betsy-devos-south-dakota-sioux-falls/4746906002/

13. For example, see Zemsky, R., Wegner, G. and Massey, M. (2005). *Remaking the American University: Market-Smart and Mission-Centered.* New Brunswick: Rutgers University Press; Zemsky, R. and Shaman, S. (2017). *The Market Imperative: Segmentation and Change in Higher Education.* Baltimore: Johns Hopkins University Press.

14. The term 'academic capitalism' derives from Slaughter, S. and L. Leslie (1999). *Academic Capitalism: Politics, Policies, and the Entrepreneurial University.* Baltimore, MD: Johns Hopkins University Press. Also see Slaughter, S. and Rhoades, G. (2009). *Academic Capitalism and the New Economy: Markets, State, and Higher Education.* Baltimore: Johns Hopkins University Press.

15. In June 2019 pro-Trump Republican Governor of Alaska Mike Dunleavy announced he intended to cut Alaska University's funding by 40 per cent, effectively bankrupting the organisation. This was eventually reduced to 21 per cent. The cuts followed Donald Trump's threat to halt federal funding to colleges who were 'hostile' to conservative viewpoints. See Brown, S. (2019). 'Here's Why Alaska's Governor Thinks His University System Needs Steep Cuts – and

Why Experts Say He's Wrong'. *The Chronicle of Higher Education*. Available at www.chronicle.com/article/Here-s-Why-Alaska-s/246779

16. House of Commons (2019). 'Higher Education Funding in England'. Available at https://researchbriefings.parliament.uk/ResearchBriefing/Summary/CBP-7973

17. Schram, S. (ed.) (2016). 'The Future of American Higher Education and Democracy: Introduction'. In *Neoliberalizing the University: Implications for American Democracy*. New York: Routledge, pp. 1–13.

18. In Ripley, A. (2018). 'Why Is College in America So Expensive?' *The Atlantic Monthly*. Available at www.theatlantic.com/education/archive/2018/09/why-is-college-so-expensive-in-america/569884/

19. Nova, A. (2019). 'College Graduates Owe $29,000 in Student Debt Now – More Than Ever Before'. *CNBC*. Available at www.cnbc.com/2019/09/19/student-debt-continues-to-climb-heres-how-much-graduates-now-owe.html

20. Hamburger, P. (2019). 'Stop Feeding College Bureaucratic Bloat'. *Wall Street Journal*. Available at www.wsj.com/articles/stop-feeding-college-bureaucratic-bloat-11559507310

21. See Staddon, J. (2019). 'Administrative Bloat: Where Does It Come From and What Is It Doing?' *The James G. Martin Center for Academic Renewal*. Available at www.jamesgmartin.center/2019/06/administrative-bloat-where-does-it-come-from-and-what-is-it-doing/

22. For example, see Rivera, L.A. (2016). *Pedigree: How Elite Students Get Elite Jobs*. Princeton: Princeton University Press.

23. For revealing statistics about the elite composition of US colleges, see *New York Times* (2017). 'Some Colleges Have More Students from the Top 1 Percent Than the Bottom 60'. Available at www.nytimes.com/interactive/2017/01/18/upshot/some-colleges-have-more-students-from-the-top-1-percent-than-the-bottom-60.html. For an extended analysis, see Golden, D. (2007). *Price of Admission: How America's Ruling Class Buys Its Way into Elite Colleges*. New York: Broadway Books. Regarding the UK situation (drawing on a Freedom of Information Act order submitted by David Lammy MP), see Richardson, H. (2017). 'Oxbridge Uncovered: More Elitist Than We Thought'. *BBC*. Available at www.bbc.com/news/education-41664459

24. Milbank, D. (2001). 'Bush Embraces Yale in Graduation Speech'. *Washington Post*. Available at www.washingtonpost.com/archive/

politics/2001/05/22/bush-embraces-yale-in-graduation-speech/13879d2a-48dd-4c7d-b7f9-8cd7b15ea9f2/

25. Brunet, R. (2019). 'French University Student's Self-immolation Sparks Anger Over Living Conditions'. *France 24*. Available at www.france24.com/en/20191114-french-university-student-s-self-immolation-sparks-anger-over-living-conditions

26. For an example of how this intersected with the pre-modern UK system in the nineteenth century, see Newman, J.H. (1852/1982). *The Idea of a University Defined*. Notre Dame: University of Notre Dame Press.

27. See Weber, 'Science as a Vocation'.

28. Barrow, C.W. (1990). *Universities and the Capitalist State: Corporate Liberalism and the Reconstruction of American Higher Education, 1894–1928*. Madison: University of Wisconsin Press.

29. See Jencks, C. and Riesman, D. (1968). *The Academic Revolution*. New York: Doubleday; Hook, S., Kurtz, P. and Todorovich, M. (eds) (1974). *The Idea of the Modern University*. Buffalo, NY: Prometheus Books.

30. Committee on Higher Education (1963). 'Higher education: Report of the Committee appointed by the Prime Minister under the Chairmanship of Lord Robbins 1961–63'. Cmnd – 2154. London: HMSO, p. 8.

31. See Washburn, J. (2005). *University, Inc: The Corporate Corruption of Higher Education*. New York: Basic Books.

32. Barcan, R. (2018). 'Life Choices: Vocation in a Casualised Work World'. *Sydney Review of Books*. Available at https://sydneyreviewofbooks.com/review/how-to-be-an-academic-inger-mewburn/. Similar research has found it's better for your mental wellbeing to be employed in a job with no 'calling' rather than one in which it goes unanswered. See Gazica, M.W. and Spector, P.E. (2015). 'A Comparison of Individuals with Unanswered Callings to Those with No Calling At All.' *Journal of Vocational Behavior*. 91: 1–10.

CHAPTER 2

1. Lewis, N. and Shore, C. (2017). 'Managing the Third Mission: Reform or Reinvention of the Public University?' In S. Wright and C. Shore (eds), *Death of the Public University? Uncertain Futures for*

Higher Education in the Knowledge Economy. Berghahn Books: New York, pp. 47–68.

2. For an example of this, see Sowell, T. (2010). *Intellectuals and Society*. New York: Basic Books.

3. Readings, *The University in Ruins*; Ginsberg, B. (2014). *The Fall of the Faculty: The Rise of the All-Administrative University and Why It Matters*. New York: Oxford University Press.

4. For example, see Aronowitz, *The Knowledge Factory*; Sommer, J.W. (ed.) (1995). *The Academy in Crisis: Political Economy of Higher Education*. New York: Routledge; Palfreyman, D. and Tapper, T. (2014). *Reshaping the University: The Rise of the Regulated Market in Higher Education*. Oxford: Oxford University Press.

5. Hill, *Whackademia*.

6. See Venugopal, R. (2015). 'Neoliberalism as a Concept'. *Economy and Society*. 44(2): 165–87.

7. For two excellent introductions, see Harvey, D. (2005). *A Brief History of Neoliberalism*. Oxford: Oxford University Press; Mirowski, P. (2014). *Never Let a Serious Crisis Go to Waste: How Neoliberalism Survived the Financial Meltdown*. London: Verso.

8. As Hardt and Negri (2019) point out, notwithstanding recent resurgences in ethno-nationalism and political populism, the transnational capitalist elite has not lessened its influence but 'merely receded from view and become less legible, as if they had discovered an invisibility potion'. Thus we need to study the various levels of neoliberalism, and its complex interconnections with an evolving and highly politicised state apparatus. Hardt, M. and Negri, A. (2019). 'Empire, Twenty Years On'. *New Left Review*. 120: 67–92, p. 92.

9. Ginsberg, *The Fall of the Faculty*.

10. For an extended discussion of this, see Marginson, S. and Considine, M. (2000). *The Enterprise University: Power, Governance and Reinvention in Australia*. Cambridge: Cambridge University Press.

11. See Lukianoff and Haidt, *The Coddling of the American Mind*.

12. Fabricant, M. and Brier, S. (2016). *Austerity Blues: Fighting for the Soul of Public Higher Education*. Baltimore: Johns Hopkins University Press.

13. For example, in their study of mental disorders among Belgium doctoral students, Levecque, Anseel, De Beuckelaer, Van der Heyden and Gisle (2017) found that 'organizational policies were significantly associated with the prevalence of mental health problems. Especially

work-family interface, job demands and job control, the supervisor's leadership style, team decision-making culture, and perception of a career outside academia are linked to mental health problems'. Levecque, K., Anseel, F., De Beuckelaer, A., Van der Heyden, J. and Gisle, L. (2017). 'Work Organization and Mental Health Problems in PhD Students'. *Research Policy.* 46(4): 868–79.

14. American Psychological Association (2018). 'One in Three College Freshmen Worldwide Reports Mental Health Disorder'. Available at www.apa.org/news/press/releases/2018/09/freshmen-mental-health

15. Ewens, H. (2019). 'How More Than 12 Students at One University Ended up Dead by Suicide'. *Vice.* Available at www.vice.com/en_uk/article/zmjq7x/how-more-than-12-students-at-one-university-ended-up-dead-by-suicide

16. Day, R. (2018). 'Exclusion under the Fitness to Study Policy'. *Epigram.* Available at https://epigram.org.uk/2018/04/27/exclusion-under-the-fitness-to-study-policy/

17. Joseph, S. (2019). 'Depression, Anxiety Rising among U.S. College Students'. *Reuters.* Available at www.reuters.com/article/us-health-mental-undergrads/depression-anxiety-rising-among-us-college-students-idUSKCN1VJ25Z

18. Fortinsky, S. and Liu, M. (2018). 'U. Officials Were Told Nine Times of Kong's Suicidal Thoughts Before Her Death, Lawsuit Says'. *The Daily Pennsylvanian.* Available at www.thedp.com/article/2018/04/olivia-kong-death-suicide-upenn-mental-health-lawsuit-university-pennsylvania-penn-philadelphia

19. Evans, T., Bira, L., Gastelum, J., Weiss, L.T. and Vanderford, N.L., (2018). 'Evidence for a Mental Health Crisis in Graduate Education'. *Nature Biotechnology.* 36: 282–4.

20. Woolston, C. (2018). 'Feeling Overwhelmed by Academia? You Are Not Alone'. *Nature.* Available at www.nature.com/articles/d41586-018-04998-1

21. The Graduate Assembly (2014). 'Graduate Student Happiness & Well-Being Report: University of Berkeley'. Available at http://ga.berkeley.edu/wp-content/uploads/2015/04/wellbeingreport_2014.pdf

22. See Hatton, E. (2020). *Coerced: Work Under Threat of Punishment.* Berkeley: University of California Press.

23. Obrien, T. and Guiney, D. (2019). 'Staff Wellbeing in Higher Education'. *Education Support Partnership.* Available at www.

    educationsupportpartnership.org.uk/resources/research-reports/
    staff-wellbeing-higher-education

24. Fazackerley, A. (2019). 'It's Cut-Throat': Half of UK Academics Stressed and 40% Thinking of Leaving'. *Guardian*. Available at www.theguardian.com/education/2019/may/21/cut-throat-half-academics-stressed-thinking-leaving?

25. Richardson, H. (2019). 'University Counselling Services "Inundated by Stressed Academics"'. *BBC*. Available at www.bbc.com/news/education-48353331

26. Tavernier, J. (2019). 'The Problem with Benchmarking'. Available at www.jodetavernier.com/2019/07/the-problem-with-benchmarking/

27. Morrish, L. (2019). 'The University Has Become an Anxiety Machine'. *Higher Education Policy Institute*. Available at www.hepi.ac.uk/2019/05/23/the-university-has-become-an-anxiety-machine/

28. Morrish, L. (2019). 'Pressure Vessels: The Epidemic of Poor Mental Health among Higher Education Staff'. *Higher Education Policy Institute*. Available at www.hepi.ac.uk/wp-content/uploads/2019/05/HEPI-Pressure-Vessels-Occasional-Paper-20.pdf

29. As Josh Hall notes, these 'wellness programmes' use the language of care to disguise managerial preoccupations with productivity and performance: 'the businesses involved are not addressing the strains and psychic dangers of the workplace by taking action to prevent them, but rather by simply treating the symptoms'. Hall, J. (2018). 'Downward-Facing Capitalist Dogma'. *The Baffler*. Available at https://thebaffler.com/latest/downward-dogma-hall

30. Times Higher Education (2016). 'UCU Report: "Academics Work Two Days a Week Unpaid"'. Available at www.timeshighereducation.com/news/ucu-report-academics-work-two-days-week-unpaid

31. Mintz, L. (2017). 'Overworked Lecturers Who Sleep in Their Offices Threatened with Disciplinary Action'. *Telegraph*. Available at www.telegraph.co.uk/education/2017/07/30/overworked-lecturers-sleep-offices-threatened-disciplinary-action/

32. Childress, H. (2019). *The Adjunct Underclass: How America's Colleges Betrayed Their Faculty, Their Students, and Their Mission*. Chicago: University of Chicago Press. For an interesting interpretation of the effect casualisation has had on university culture, see Donoghue, F. (2018). *The Last Professors: The Corporate University and the Fate of the Humanities*. New York: Fordham University Press.

33. Of course, it goes without saying that everyone is ultimately less productive as a result. One can only be effective for so long, with

anything over 50 hours a week pretty much wasted effort or worse. This introduces yet another depressing dimension into the neoliberal university. What if all this work is actually hindering our ability to be productive teachers and researchers?

34. Lee, O. (2015). 'I Have One of the Best Jobs in Academia. Here's Why I'm Walking Away.' *Vox*. Available at www.vox.com/2015/9/8/9261531/professor-quitting-job

35. Ibid.

36. hooks, b. (1994). *Teaching to Transgress: Education as the Practice of Freedom*. New York: Routledge.

37. Gannon, *Radical Hope*, p. 2.

38. Worthington, E. and Taylor, K. (2019). 'Four Corners Whistleblower Sued by Murdoch University after Raising Concerns About International Students'. *Australian Broadcasting Corporation*. Available at www.abc.net.au/news/2019-10-11/murdoch-university-sues-four-corners-whistleblower/11591520

39. Australian Productivity Commission (2019). 'Mental Health'. Available at www.pc.gov.au/inquiries/current/mental-health/draft/mental-health-draft-volume2.pdf

40. Marinetto, M. (2019). 'Modern Universities Are Not Neoliberal – But Many Academics Are'. *Times Higher Education*. Available at www.timeshighereducation.com/opinion/modern-universities-are-not-neoliberal-many-academics-are

41. As Carl Rhodes astutely notes, academic freedom has nothing to do with staff being exempt from departmental responsibilities or doing whatever they want. The idea instead means that universities (and the knowledge they produce) ought to be free from external interference from the state, church, business, etc. Academic freedom originates from a long struggle and is a founding principle of modern higher education. That it has been recast in such individualistic terms is telling of how market ideology has commandeered individual agency in the occupation, typically to the detriment of the profession as a whole. See Rhodes, C. (2017). 'Academic Freedom in the Corporate University: Squandering Our Inheritance?' In M. Izak, M. Kostera and M. Zawadzki (eds), *The Future of University Education*. London: Palgrave Macmillan, pp. 19–38.

42. Lukianoff and Haidt, *The Coddling of the American Mind*.

43. For example, Gary Rolf argues that while corporatisation has been thoroughgoing, there are still ways to thrive within the ruins, secret spaces where we can still do what we love in an ever hostile envi-

ronment. I will argue later that this strategy is doomed. Rolf, G. (2013). *The University in Dissent: Scholarship in the Corporate University*. London: Routledge and the Society for Research into Higher Education.

44. Harney, S. and Moten, F. (2013). *The Undercommons: Fugitive Planning & Black Study*. New York: Minor Compositions.

CHAPTER 3

1. See Collini, S. (2012). *What Are Universities For?* London: Penguin; Giroux, H. (2014). *Neoliberalism's Attack on Higher Education*. New York: Haymarket Books; Aronowitz, *The Knowledge Factory*.

2. Washburn, *University, Inc.*

3. Which is sadly ironic. Numerous studies indicate that humanities and social science graduates are employed at the same rate as STEM degree holders. For example, see *The British Academy* (2020). *Qualified for the Future: Quantifying Demand for Arts, Humanities and Social Science Skills*. London: British Academy.

4. For excellent analyses of this contradiction, see Martin, R. (2012). *Under New Management: Universities, Administrative Labor, and the Professional Turn*. Philadelphia: Temple University Press; Nelson, C. (2010). *No University Is an Island: Saving Academic Freedom*. New York and London: New York University Press.

5. As Ruth Barcan (2018) outlines, the vocational component of academic labour explains why the malaise is deeper than simple work-life balance problems. A vocational calling 'not only speaks to the "passionate attachment" that academic labour shares with (other) creative labour but also places duty, commitment, faith and hope at the centre. This much older discourse thus helps us recognise contemporary academic professional ambivalence not only as a typical and widespread late-modern concern about "work-life balance" or personal job satisfaction, but also as a fundamental values conflict about the increasing individual cost of contributing to the public good.' Barcan, R. (2018) 'Paying Dearly for Privilege: Conceptions, Experiences and Temporalities of Vocation in Academic Life.' *Pedagogy, Culture & Society*. 26(1): 105–21, p. 108.

6. See Collini, S. (2017). *Speaking of Universities*. London: Verso.

7. As Brian Pusser and Dudley Doane point out, 'a key distinction between the nonprofit and for-profit production of higher education

is that for-profit providers are fundamentally orientated to the pro-duction of a private benefit: enhanced labour-market outcomes for individuals. While nonprofits are also committed to producing that benefit, their missions have long incorporated the production of public benefits as well. Moreover, in their institutional behaviour, non-profit institutions have justified public subsidy by focusing on public benefits – for example, long term research that contributes to basic knowledge, community service, and liberal education over commercial activities.' Pusser, B. and Doane, D.J. (2001). 'Public Purpose and Private Enterprise.' *Change.* 33(5): 19–22, p. 21.

8. It must be noted, however, that this emulation of big business falls *well short* of the material trappings associated with big business, in all but the elite institutions at least. For example, few academics fly business class to conferences, with the exception of senior managers. Indeed, if you want to provoke the ire of university administra-tion, then mention business class travel and their disdain becomes palpable. It's not simply a question of expenditure. Even academics with sufficient funds will be censured for having the audacity to book anything other than bargain-bin fares. The contempt is more to do with status and the belief that public sector employees are techni-cally unworthy, no matter how successful they are as academics. In most cases, the nominal 'corporate university' adopts corporatisation of a very specific kind (a poor man's version if you like), one that quickly evokes the discourse of 'public austerity' and 'budgetary con-straints' as the situation requires.

9. Wright and Shore, *Death of the Public University?*

10. See Hood, C. (1995). 'The "New Public Management" in the 1980s: Variations on a Theme'. *Accounting, Organization and Society.* 20(2/3): 93–109; Paradeise, C. Reale, E., Bleiklie, I. and Ferlie, E. (eds) (2009). *University Governance: Western European Comparative Perspectives.* London: Springer.

11. Public Choice Theory is a branch of neoclassical economics that views state bureaucrats as rent-seeking utility maximisers. It assumes that public servants are just as greedy as capitalists, but enjoy an unfair advantage due to their monopoly privileges, which are exploited to the broader detriment of society. Following the left-wing revolts in US colleges (including his own UCLA) in the late 1960s, the deeply conservative James M. Buchanan vengefully aimed Public Choice Theory at universities in *Academia in Anarchy* (co-authored with Nicos E. Devletoglou). He hated free education because it

distorted the price mechanism and sent the wrong signals to rebellious students and left-leaning professors. Buchanan imagined a car factory operating under the same principles, cranking out substandard Lada-like degrees. We need capitalist plants instead in higher education, he averred. As such degrees ought to be treated as private commodities like any other: 'if people will so curiously insist on arguing that university education is a free good, those who demand, supply, and finance it will begin to act as if it were, in fact, free! The delusion that university education is a free good leads to disregard both for cost reduction and for efficiency in large or small matters. This is first-day economics. Yet its truth is widely denied, and institutions reflect this denial.' Buchanan, J.M. and Devletoglou, N.E. (1970). *Anarchy in Academia: An Economic Diagnosis*. New York: Basic Books, p. 6.

12. A rather disturbing example of this arose when the Vice Chancellor of Imperial College was questioned about the suicide of Professor Stefan Grimm (who we discuss in Chapter 6). She remarked, 'professors are really like small business owners ... it's a very competitive world out there'. See BBC (2015). 'Professor Alice Gast on BBC Radio 4's Today Programme'. Available at www.imperial.ac.uk/imedia/content/view/4708/professor-alice-gast-on-bbc-radio-4s-today-programme-friday-17-april-2015/

13. See Henkel, M. (2005), 'Academic Identity and Autonomy in a Changing Policy Environment'. *Higher Education*. 49(1/2): 156–7; Marginson, S. (2008). 'Academic Creativity under New Public Management: Foundations for an Investigation.' *Educational Theory*. 58(3): 269–87.

14. Shore, C. (2008). 'Audit Culture and Illiberal Governance: Universities and the Politics of Accountability'. *Anthropological Theory*. 8(3): 278–98.

15. See Hall, G. (2016). *The Uberfication of the University*. Minneapolis: University of Minnesota Press; Kezar and DePaola, *The Gig Academy*.

16. Lapsley, I. (2009). 'New Public Management: The Cruellest Invention of the Human Spirit?' *Abacus*. 45(1): 1–21.

17. For an incisive analysis of this false-history telling, see Readings, *The University in Ruins*. According to Readings, the businessification of higher education has destroyed the Fichtean axiom that the university exists to 'inculcate the exercise of critical judgment'

and consequently 'no longer participates in its historical project for humanity'. Ibid., pp. 5–6.

18. Brennan, J. and Magness, P. (2019). *Cracks in the Ivory Tower: The Moral Mess of Higher Education*. New York: Oxford University Press.

19. Ibid., pp. 9–10.

20. An article penned by an anonymous academic describes an encounter with a commissioning editor in the monograph industry. When the editor phoned and asked him/her to write a book the academic asked what the retail price would be: £80, they were told. The editor (one of many in his company) then confessed s/he needed to commission 75 monographs per year and aimed to sell at least 300 copies each to libraries around the world, amounting to £1.8 million. The anonymous academic concluded, 'I'd been asked to write a book about whatever I wanted, and this editor didn't even know whether I'd written anything before. It didn't matter. It would sell its 300 copies regardless. Not to people with an interest in reading the book, but to librarians who would put it on a shelf and then, a few years later, probably bury it in a storeroom.' Anonymous (2015). 'Academics Are Being Hoodwinked into Writing Books Nobody Can Buy'. *Guardian*. Available at www.theguardian.com/higher-education-network/2015/sep/04/academics-are-being-hoodwinked-into-writing-books-nobody-can-buy

21. Childress, *The Adjunct Underclass*.

22. Kilganon, C. (2014). 'Without Tenure or a Home.' *New York Times*. Available at www.nytimes.com/2014/03/30/nyregion/without-tenure-or-a-home.html

23. Wright, R. (2019). 'Five English Universities Paid Their Heads More Than £500,000'. *Financial Times*. Available at www.ft.com/content/cafdc39a-2eb5-11e9-ba00-0251022932c8

24. See Sauntson, H. and Morrish, L. (2011). 'Vision, Values, and International Excellence: The "Products" That University Mission Statements Sell to Students.' In M. Molesworth, R. Scullion and E. Nixon (eds), *The Marketisation of Higher Education and the Student as Consumer*. London: Routledge, pp. 73–85.

25. La Berge, C. (2019). 'A Market Correction in the Humanities – What Are You Going to Do with That?' *Los Angeles Review of Books*. Available at https://lareviewofbooks.org/article/a-market-correction-in-the-humanities-what-are-you-going-to-do-with-that/

26. McGettigan, A. and Adams, R. (2019). 'Reading University in Crisis amid Questions over £121m Land Sales'. *Guardian*. Available at

www.theguardian.com/education/2019/feb/09/reading-university-in-crisis-amid-questions-over-121m-land-sales

27. Gill, R. (2009). 'Breaking the Silence: The Hidden Injuries of Neo-Liberal Academia'. In R. Flood and R. Gill (eds), *Secrecy and Silence in the Research Process: Feminist Reflections*. London: Routledge, pp. 228–44.

CHAPTER 4

1. Warner, M. (2014). 'Why I Quit'. *London Review of Books*. 36(17). Available at www.lrb.co.uk/the-paper/v36/n17/marina-warner/diary

2. See Spitzer, R. (2012). 'The Disappearing Faculty'. *HuffPost*. Available at www.huffpost.com/entry/the-disappearing-faculty_b_1240204

3. American Institute for Research (2014). 'Is "Admin Bloat" Behind the High Cost of College?' Available at www.air.org/resource/admin-bloat-behind-high-cost-college

4. New England Center for Investigative Reporting (2014). 'New Analysis Shows Problematic Boom in Higher Ed Administrators'. Available at www.necir.org/2014/02/06/new-analysis-shows-problematic-boom-in-higher-ed-administrators/

5. Times Higher Education (2015). 'Academics in the Minority at More Than Two-Thirds of UK Universities'. Available at www.timeshighereducation.com/news/academics-minority-more-two-thirds-uk-universities

6. See Churcher, M. and Talbot, D. (2020). 'The Corporatization of Education: Bureaucracy, Boredom and Transformative Possibilities'. *New Formations*. 100–1: 28–42.

7. Ginsberg, *The Fall of the Faculty*, p. 2.

8. I have borrowed the term 'sludge' from Herd, P. and Moynihan, D.P. (2018). *Administrative Burden: Policy Making by Other Means*. New York: Russell Sage Foundation.

9. See Adler, P.S. and Borys, B. (1996). 'Two Types of Bureaucracy: Enabling and Coercive'. *Administrative Science Quarterly*. 41: 61–89.

10. See McKie, A. (2020). 'Covid-19: Universities Treating Staff in "Vastly Different Ways"'. *Times Higher Education*. Available at www.timeshighereducation.com/news/covid-19-universities-treating-staff-vastly-different-ways

11. Gordon, D. (1996). *Fat and Mean: The Corporate Squeeze of Working Americans and the Myth of Managerial 'Downsizing'*. New York: Free Press, p. 40.

12. Employment contracts and contracts-for-services are not new, of course. But what might be termed the process of *contractualisation*, however, refers to the application of neoclassical economics to the legal precepts of employment, as epitomised in the writings of Richard A. Epstein. It's hastened the hyper-individualisation of work and helped dismantle the collectivism associated with trade unions, national labour legislation (e.g., the National Labor Relations Act in the US) and industry-wide awards. See Epstein, A.R. (1983). 'Common Law for Labor Relations: A Critique of the New Deal Labor Legislation'. *Yale Law Journal*. 92(8): 1357–408; Epstein, R.A. (1984). 'In Defense of Contract at Will'. *The University of Chicago Law Review*. 51: 947–82.

13. In this respect, Stewart Clegg and John McAuley point out that we ought to avoid the managerial vs collegiate dualism since there are a wide range of subject positions that non-academic staff take in the corporate university. Clegg, S. and McAuley, J. (2005). 'Conceptualising Middle Management in Higher Education: A Multifaceted Discourse'. *Journal of Higher Education Policy and Management*. 27(1): 19–34.

14. Keltner, D. (2016). 'Don't Let Power Corrupt You'. *Harvard Business Review*. October, 112–15.

15. Keltner nicely demonstrates this with his 'cookie monster' lab experiment. Three people are given a task to complete. One is randomly assigned the role of 'leader'. Midway through the experiment a plate of four freshly baked cookies is placed in the room as a reward, one for each member plus an additional cookie. Keltner asks, 'who would take a second treat knowing it would deprive the others of the same? It was nearly always the person who had been named the leader. In addition, the leader was more likely to eat with their mouths open, lips smacking and crumbs falling on their clothes.' Ibid., p. 113.

16. Keltner, D. (2016). *The Power Paradox: How We Gain and Lose Influence*. New York: Penguin.

17. Mathews, D. (2018). 'If You Love Research, Academia May Not Be for You'. *Times Higher Education*. Available at www.timeshigher education.com/blog/if-you-love-research-academia-may-not-be-you

18. See Bicudo de Castro, V. (2017). 'Unpacking the Notion of Subjectivity: Performance Evaluation and Supervisor Discretion'. *The British Accounting Review.* 49(6): 532–44.

19. For an excellent analysis of this, see West, D. (2016). 'The Managerial University: A Failed Experiment?' *Demos.* Available at http://demosjournal.com/the-managerial-university-a-failed-experiment/

20. Srigley, R. (2018). 'Whose University Is It Anyway?' *Los Angeles Review of Books.* Available at https://lareviewofbooks.org/article/whose-university-is-it-anyway/#_edn1

21. Traynor, L. (2014). 'Top Professor Suspended by University for "Sighing" and Giving Off "Negative Vibes"'. *Mirror.* Available at www.mirror.co.uk/news/uk-news/top-professor-suspended-university-sighing-4498375

22. Delvin, H. and Marsh, S. (2018o). 'Hundreds of Academics at Top UK Universities Accused of Bullying'. *Guardian.* Available at www.theguardian.com/education/2018/sep/28/academics-uk-universities-accused-bullying-students-colleagues

23. Skinner, P., Peetz, D., Strachan, G., Whitehouse, G., Bailey, J. and Broadbent, K. (2015). 'Self-reported Harassment and Bullying in Australian Universities: Explaining Differences between Regional, Metropolitan and Elite Institutions'. *The Journal of Higher Education Policy and Management.* 37(5): 558–71.

24. West, 'The Managerial University'.

25. Research by Hollis (2015) found that in US universities, 'workplace bullying often comes from leadership and that human resources seldom advocated for the target, leaving the target toiling in isolation, disengaging from organizational objectives, or leaving the organization'. Hollis, L.P. (2015). 'Bully University? The Cost of Workplace Bullying and Employee Disengagement in American Higher Education'. *SAGE Open.* https://doi.org/10.1177/2158244015589997

26. Research confirms that perceptions of HR vary depending on whether managers are asked (who are generally very positive) or employees (who typically experience HR in a negative manner). Given the power relations in management-led organisations like the university, their views generally hold sway, further deepening the disconnect between workers and senior officials. See Wang, Y., Kim, S., Rafferty, A. and Sanders, K. (2019). 'Employee Perceptions of HR Practices: A Critical Review and Future Directions'. *The International Journal of Human Resource Management.* 31(1): 128–73.

27. King, M. (2011). 'HR: Your Friend or Your Foe?' *Guardian*. Available at www.theguardian.com/money/2011/may/28/hr-friend-or-foe-human-resources

28. Croxford, R. (2019). 'UK Universities Face "Gagging Order" Criticism'. *BBC*. Available at www.bbc.com/news/education-4793 6662

29. Ibid.

30. Fisher analyses this in relation to his own depression: 'each member of the subordinate class is encouraged into feeling that their poverty, lack of opportunities, or unemployment is their fault and their fault alone'. Fisher, M. (2018). *K-Punk: The Collected and Unpublished Writings of Mark Fisher (2004–2016)*. London: Repeater Books, p. 749.

31. For analyses of these dynamics in the US, see Cabrera, N. L (2018). *White Guys on Campus: Racism, White Immunity and the Myth of 'Post-Racial' Higher Education*. New Brunswick: Rutgers University Press. Concerning racism in UK universities, see Arday, J. and Safia Mirza, H. (2018). *Dismantling Race in Higher Education: Racism, Whiteness and Decolonising the Academy*. London: Palgrave Macmillan.

CHAPTER 5

1. Muller, J.Z. (2018). *The Tyranny of Metrics*. Princeton: Princeton University Press.

2. Jarratt Report (1985). 'Report of the Steering Committee for Efficiency Studies in Universities Committee of Vice-Chancellors and Principals'. Available at www.educationengland.org.uk/documents/jarratt1985/index.html

3. Marilyn Strathern (ed.) (2000). *Audit Cultures: Anthropological Studies in Accountability, Ethics and the Academy*. London: Routledge.

4. Lorenz, C. (2012). 'If You're So Smart, Why Are You Under Surveillance? Universities, Neoliberalism and New Public Management'. *Critical Inquiry*. 38(3): 599–629.

5. Beer, D. (2018). *The Data Gaze: Capitalism, Power and Perception*. London: Sage.

6. Hussain, S. (2016). 'A Web of Cyber Controversy: UC Monitoring of Campus Network Traffic Sparks Outrage among Faculty'. *The Daily Californian*. Available at www.dailycal.org/2016/02/02/web-cyber-controversy/

7. Brandist, C. (2014). 'A Very Stalinist Management Model'. *Times Higher Education*. Available at www.timeshighereducation.com/comment/opinion/a-very-stalinist-management-model/2013616. article

8. Siegelbaum, L.H. (1990). *Stakhanovism and the Politics of Productivity in the USSR, 1935–1941*. Cambridge: Cambridge University Press.

9. Muller, J.Z. (2018). 'Against Metrics: How Measuring Performance by Numbers Backfires'. *Aeon*. Available at https://aeon.co/ideas/against-metrics-how-measuring-performance-by-numbers-backfires

10. Also see Vostal, F. (2016). *Accelerating Academia: The Changing Structure of Academic Time*. London: Palgrave Macmillan.

11. Kantor, J. and Streitfeld, D. (2015). 'Inside Amazon: Wrestling Big Ideas in a Bruising Workplace'. *New York Times*. Available at www.nytimes.com/2015/08/16/technology/inside-amazon-wrestling-big-ideas-in-a-bruising-workplace.html

12. See ter Bogt, H.J. and Scapens, R.W. (2012). 'Performance Management in Universities: Effects of the Transition to More Quantitative Measurement Systems'. *European Accounting Review*. 21(3): 451–97.

13. Espeland, W.N. and Sauder, M. (2016). *Engines of Anxiety: Academic Rankings, Reputation and Accountability*. New York: Russell Sage Foundation.

14. Ibid., p. 4.

15. Vann, M. (2003). 'Of Rats, Rice, and Race: The Great Hanoi Rat Massacre'. *French Colonial History*. 4: 193–204.

16. Flitter, E. and Cowley, S. (2019). 'Wells Fargo Says Its Culture Has Changed: Some Employees Disagree'. *New York Times*. Available at www.nytimes.com/2019/03/09/business/wells-fargo-sales-culture.html

17. Bunge, N. (2018). 'Students Evaluating Teachers Doesn't Just Hurt Teachers – It Hurts Students'. *The Chronicle of Higher Education*. Available at www.chronicle.com/article/Students-Evaluating-Teachers/245169

18. Edwards, M. and Roy, S. (2015). 'Academic Research in the 21st Century: Maintaining Scientific Integrity in a Climate of Perverse Incentives and Hypercompetition'. *Environmental Engineering Science*. 34(1): 51–61.

19. Also see Abbott, A., Cyranoski, D., Jones, N., Maher, B., Schiermeier, Q. and Van Noorden, R. (2010). 'Do Metrics Matter?' *Nature.* 465: 860–2.
20. Edwards and Roy, 'Academic Research in the 21st Century', p. 52.
21. Ibid.
22. Monbiot, G. (2011). 'Academic Publishers Make Murdoch Look Like a Socialist'. *Guardian.* Available at www.theguardian.com/commentisfree/2011/aug/29/academic-publishers-murdoch-socialist
23. See Head, M.L., Holman, L., Lanfear, R., Kahn, A.T. and Jennions, M.D. (2015). 'The Extent and Consequences of P-Hacking in Science'. *PLoS Biology.* 13(3). Available at www.ncbi.nlm.nih.gov/pmc/articles/PMC4359000/
24. See Enserink (2012). 'Final Report: Stapel Affair Points to Bigger Problems in Social Psychology'. *Science.* Available at www.sciencemag.org/news/2012/11/final-report-stapel-affair-points-bigger-problems-social-psychology

CHAPTER 6

1. Specia, M. (2019). 'How Did We Miss Him? Student Death Prompts Inquiries in New Zealand'. *New York Times.* Available at www.nytimes.com/2019/09/26/world/australia/new-zealand-student-death.html
2. Russell, E. (2019). 'Dead for Weeks: University Campus Services Provider Promise Thorough Investigation of What Went Wrong'. *New Zealand Herald.* Available at www.nzherald.co.nz/nz/news/article.cfm?c_id=1&objectid=12271212
3. Ibid.
4. Specia, 'How Did We Miss Him?'
5. As mentioned earlier, for a prominent example, see Lukianoff and Haidt, *The Coddling of the American Mind.*
6. New Zealand Herald (2019). 'University of Canterbury Death: Mason Pendrous' Stepfather's Warning over Scam Fundraising Page'. Available at www.nzherald.co.nz/nz/news/article.cfm?c_id=1&objectid=12277394
7. Anonymous (2018). 'Loneliness on Campus'. *Honi Soit.* Available at https://honisoit.com/2018/10/loneliness-on-campus/
8. See Valbrun, M. (2020). 'Academics Lost to Covid-19 Fondly Remembered'. *Inside Higher Ed.* Available at www.insidehighered.

com/news/2020/04/15/academics-lost-covid-19-fondly-remembered

9. Griffith, J. (2019). 'Head of Mental Health Services at University of Pennsylvania Dies by Suicide'. *NBC News*. Available at www.nbc news.com/news/us-news/head-mental-health-services-university-pennsylvania-dies-suicide-n1052156

10. Snyder, S., Newell, M. and Dean, M. (2019). 'Penn's Head of Counseling and Psychological Services Dies by Suicide at Center City Building'. *Philadelphia Inquirer*. Available at www.inquirer. com/news/unviersity-of-pennsylvania-death-psychological-services-20190909.html

11. Ibid.

12. Liu, M. and Cohen, M. (2019). 'CAPS Executive Director Gregory Eells Died by Suicide Monday Morning'. *The Daily Pennsylvanian*. Available at www.thedp.com/article/2019/09/caps-director-gregory-eells-dies-penn

13. Snyder, Newell and Dean, 'Penn's Head of Counseling'.

14. Ibid.

15. Babcock, L. and Saul. J. (2014). 'Dad: Stress Drove UPenn Track Star to Suicide'. *New York Post*. Available at https://nypost. com/2014/01/20/dad-track-star-killed-self-over-stress-from-upenn-workload/

16. Stancliffe-Cook, M. (2019). 'Chemistry Student Dies Suddenly in 13th Suspected Suicide at Bristol University in Three Years'. *Independent*. Available at www.independent.co.uk/news/uk/home-news/student-death-suicide-bristol-university-maria-stancliffe-cook-a9051606.html

17. Cohen, S. and Italiano, L. (2017). 'Suicide Wave Grips Columbia'. *New York Post*. Available at https://nypost.com/2017/02/02/suicide-wave-grips-columbia/

18. Stuckler, D. and Basu, S. (2013). *The Body Economic: Why Austerity Kills*. New York: Alan Lane.

19. BBC (2019). 'France Telecom Suicides: Former Bosses Go on Trial'. Available at www.bbc.com/news/business-48175938

20. Purdy, S. (2019). 'Statement Following Inquest of Ben Murray'. Available at www.bristol.ac.uk/news/2019/may/statement-following-the-inquest-of-ben-murray.html

21. See Leader, D. (2008). *The New Black: Mourning, Melancholy and Depression*. London: Penguin.

22. Parr, C. (2014). 'Imperial College Professor Stefan Grimm "Was Given Grant Income Target"'. *Times Higher Education*. Available at www.timeshighereducation.com/news/imperial-college-professor-stefan-grimm-was-given-grant-income-target/2017369.article

23. DC's Improbable Science (2014) 'Publish *and* Perish at Imperial College London: The Death of Stefan Grimm'. Available at www.dcscience.net/2014/12/01/publish-and-perish-at-imperial-college-london-the-death-of-stefan-grimm/

24. Krause, G. (2018). 'We Must Confront the Culture of Overwork to Tackle Academia's Mental Health Crisis'. *Times Higher Education*. Available at www.timeshighereducation.com/blog/we-must-confront-culture-overwork-tackle-academias-mental-health-crisis

25. Jones, C.H. (2019). 'Lecturer's Widow Hits Out at Cardiff University Workload'. *BBC*. Available at www.bbc.com/news/uk-wales-47296631

26. Walford, J. (2018). 'University Tutor Died after "Silently Struggling" with Workload'. *Wales Online*. Available at www.walesonline.co.uk/news/wales-news/university-tutor-died-after-silently-14751533

27. Krause, 'We Must Confront the Culture of Overwork'.

28. Shaw, C. (2014). 'Overworked and Isolated: Work Pressure Fuels Mental Illness in Academia'. *Guardian*. Available at www.theguardian.com/higher-education-network/blog/2014/may/08/work-pressure-fuels-academic-mental-illness-guardian-study-health

29. Kovalik, D. (2019). 'Death of an Adjunct'. *Pittsburgh Post-Gazette*. Available at www.post-gazette.com/opinion/Op-Ed/2013/09/18/Death-of-an-adjunct/stories/201309180224

30. Ibid.

31. Harris, A. (2019). 'The Death of an Adjunct'. *The Atlantic*. Available at www.theatlantic.com/education/archive/2019/04/adjunct-professors-higher-education-thea-hunter/586168/

32. Frederickson, C. (2015) 'There Is No Excuse for How Universities Treat Adjuncts'. *The Atlantic*. Available at www.theatlantic.com/business/archive/2015/09/higher-education-college-adjunct-professor-salary/404461/

33. Finkelsten, M., Conley, V.M and Schuster, J. (2016). 'Taking the Measure of Faculty Diversity'. *TIAA Institute*. Available at www.tiaainstitute.org/sites/default/files/presentations/2017-02/taking_the_measure_of_faculty_diversity.pdf

34. Harris, 'The Death of an Adjunct'.

35. Ibid.

CHAPTER 7

1. Amnesty International (2019). 'Yemen: US-made Bomb Used in Deadly Air Strike on Civilians'. Available at www.amnesty.org/en/latest/news/2019/09/yemen-us-made-bomb-used-in-deadly-air-strike-on-civilians/

2. Ibid.

3. Walsh, D. (2019). 'Saudi Warplanes, Most Made in America, Still Bomb Civilians in Yemen'. *New York Times*. Available at www.nytimes.com/2019/05/22/world/middleeast/saudi-yemen-air-strikes-civilians.html

4. Elbagir, N., Abdelaziz, S., Browne, R., Arvanitidis, B. and Smith-Sparek, L. (2018). 'Bomb That Killed 40 Children in Yemen was Supplied by the US'. *CNN*. Available at https://edition.cnn.com/2018/08/17/middleeast/us-saudi-yemen-bus-strike-intl/index.html

5. Channel Four Dispatches (2019). 'Britain's Hidden War'. Available at www.channel4.com/press/news/britains-hidden-war-channel-4-dispatches

6. Raytheon (2015). 'Print a Missile: Raytheon Research Points to 3-D Printing for Tomorrow's Technology'. Available at www.raytheon.com/news/feature/print-missile

7. For example, see Aguirre, E. (2016). 'Mathematical Modelling Makes Smart Weapon's Smarter'. *UMass Lowell*. Available at www.uml.edu/news/stories/2016/avitabile-smart-weapons.aspx

8. Reidy, C. (2014). 'Raytheon, UMass Lowell Open On-campus Research Institute'. *Boston Globe*. Available at www.uml.edu/news/news-articles/2014/globe-raytheon-post.aspx

9. Doward, J. and Bennet, G. (2018). 'Defence Contractors Hand British Universities £40m'. *Observer*. Available at www.theguardian.com/world/2018/mar/31/defence-contractors-british-universities-funding

10. American Association of Universities (2019). 'Economic Impact'. Available at www.aau.edu/education-service/service/economic-impact; Research England (2019). 'REF Impact'. Available at https://re.ukri.org/research/ref-impact/; Australian Research Council (2019). 'Research Impact Principles and Framework'. Available at www.arc.gov.au/policies-strategies/strategy/research-impact-principles-framework

11. See Popp Berman, E. (2015). *Creating the Market University: How Academic Science Became an Economic Engine.* Princeton: Princeton University Press.

12. Hayek's argument is a little more complex than this, which adds a rather sinister depth to it. In fact, for him there are no 'ultimate economic ends' or 'motives': 'only in the pathological case of the miser, there is no such thing'. Economic instruments – money, debt, wages, insurance – are merely *means* for achieving a near infinite number of unspecified ends (of which, Hayek has little interest in). Such means are *universal*, however, and must be respected as such. It's this universality that then transforms monetary reason (cost/loss, returns on investment, etc.) into the sole arbiter of political, cultural and social value. Hayek, F.A. (1944). *The Road to Serfdom.* London: Routledge, p. 67.

13. Here we might also include the 'Times Higher Education Impact Ranking' which takes its cue from the United Nation's Sustainability Goals, including categories like 'Gender Equality', 'Climate Action', 'Peace, Justice and Strong Institutions' alongside, of course, 'Decent Work and Economic Growth' and 'Industry, Innovation and Infrastructure'. Times Higher Education (2019). 'University Impact Ratings 2019'. Available at www.timeshighereducation.com/rankings/impact/2019/overall#!/page/0/length/25/sort_by/rank/sort_order/asc/cols/undefined

14. For a more detailed analysis of the connection between the contemporary university, racism, war and the 'military-industrial-academic-complex', particularly in the US, see Giroux, H. (2007). *The University in Chains: Confronting the Military-Industrial-Academic Complex.* Boulder: Paradigm; also see Chatterjee, P. and Maira, S. (eds) (2014). *The Imperial University: Academic Repression and Scholarly Dissent.* Minneapolis: University of Minnesota Press.

15. Magee, A. (2019). 'A Deal with the Devil: Raytheon, UMass Lowell and a Lust for Blood'. *Massachusetts Peace Action.* Available at https://masspeaceaction.org/a-deal-with-the-devil/

16. Bentley University (2019). 'Raytheon Lectureship in Business'. Available at www.bentley.edu/centers/center-for-business-ethics/about-center/thought-leadership/raytheon-lectures

17. Biswas, A.K. and Kirchherr, J. (2015). 'Prof, No One Is Reading You'. *Straits Times.* Available at www.straitstimes.com/opinion/prof-no-one-is-reading-you

18. For example, in a similar article inspired by Biswas and Kirchherr, it's argued that 'government and university policies need to become more prescriptive in what they expect from academics ... incentives should be added to encourage academics to share their research with the general public. Doing this sort of work ought to count towards promotions and should yield rewards for both universities and individual academics.' Heleta, S. (2016). 'Academics Can Change the World – If They Stop Talking Only to Their Peers'. *The Conversation.* Available at https://theconversation.com/academics-can-change-the-world-if-they-stop-talking-only-to-their-peers-55713?

19. Reinhart, C.M. and Rogoff, K.S. (2010). 'Growth in a Time of Debt'. *American Economic Review.* 100(2): 573–8.

20. Herndon, T., Ash, M. and Pollin, R. (2014). 'Does High Public Debt Consistently Stifle Economic Growth? A Critique of Reinhart and Rogoff'. *Cambridge Journal of Economics.* 38(2): 257–79.

21. Wilson, J. and Kelling, G. (1982). 'Broken Windows'. *The Atlantic Monthly.* Available at https://media4.manhattan-institute.org/pdf/_atlantic_monthly-broken_windows.pdf

22. Roberts, D. (1999). 'Foreword: Race, Vagueness, and the Social Meaning of Order-Maintenance Policing'. *The Journal of Criminal Law and Criminology.* 89(3): 775–836.

23. For example, in 2020 the Australian government doubled the cost of humanities degrees in an effort to nudge students into job-ready STEM subjects instead. The policy was widely considered a major blow to the very idea of university education in Australia. Stuart, N. (2020). 'One of the Most Ill-Considered, Anti-Intellectual "Initiatives" Seen for Decades'. *Canberra Times.* Available at www.canberratimes.com.au/story/6803267/one-of-the-most-ill-considered-anti-intellectual-initiatives-seen-for-decades/

24. Fish, S. (2018). 'Stop Trying to Sell the Humanities', *The Chronicle of Higher Education.* Available at www.chronicle.com/article/Stop-Trying-to-Sell-the/243643

25. Schuman, R. (2013). 'Thesis Hatement: Getting a Literature Ph.D. Will Turn You into an Emotional Trainwreck, Not a Professor', *Slate.* Available at www.slate.com/articles/life/culturebox/2013/04/there_are_no_academic_jobs_and_getting_a_ph_d_will_make_you_into_a_horrible.html

26. Kay, A. (2019). 'Academe's Extinction Event: Failure, Whiskey, and Professional Collapse at the MLA'. *The Chronicle of Higher*

Education. Available at www.chronicle.com/interactives/20190510-academes-extinction-event?

27. Kay describes the scene in beautifully crafted prose: 'have you ever seen that viral picture from 2017 of a party of Oregon golfers calmly putting while, in the near distance, a wildfire consumes the landscape? Trees blacken; smoke, pinkish-gray, shrouds everything in impasto blots; nature itself seems to creak, groan, and at last give way. But the golfers go blithely on. The conversion of this Edenic place into Dantean incandescence won't interfere with the genteel game they know and love – or, if it will, they are determined to get in one last round before the region is razed. "Eye on the ball, Chet!" one can hear them saying. "Not on the cataclysm!"'

28. See Latour, B. and Woogar, S. (1979). *Laboratory Life: The Construction of Scientific Facts*. Thousand Oaks, CA: Sage.

29. See Whitley, R., Gläser, J. and Engwall, L. (eds) (2010). *Reconfiguring Knowledge Production: Changing Authority Relationships in the Sciences and Their Consequences for Intellectual Innovation*. Oxford: Oxford University Press.

30. Washburn, *University, Inc.*

31. For a recent and excellent call to arms, see Dean, J. (2019). *Comrade: An Essay on Political Belonging*. London: Verso.

32. For example, see Sowell, *Intellectuals and Society*. Sowell argues that specialised expertise (displayed by Noam Chomsky in relation to linguistics or Bertrand Russell in mathematics, for instance) confers no right to speak in the name of the people. Hence why most intellectuals end up meddling in business that isn't theirs, Sowell maintains. However, Jean-Paul Sartre confronted this very criticism back in the mid-1960s, revealing its asinine logic. Politically speaking, most intellectuals are in fact deeply conservative and uncritical, asleep at the wheel ... that's their default setting according to Sartre. Nevertheless, public intellectuals can emerge precisely due to the contradiction between their specialised practice (the particular) and wider societal structures (the universal). For example, a doctor isn't engaged in cancer research to simply enrich the wealthy 1 per cent. In her mind, *everyone* could potentially benefit from a breakthrough. But then she confronts the stark realities of the capitalist healthcare system, which contradicts the universal precept. She can either ignore the contradiction (which is almost always the case) or speak up about it, hoping to resolve it in some way. This is no deterministic process, of course. As Sartre remarks, 'every technician of knowledge

is a potential intellectual since he is defined by a contradiction which is none other than the permanent tension within him between his universalist technique and the dominant ideology. But in reality a technician cannot simply decide to become an intellectual. Such a conversion will depend in part on his personal history, which may determine whether the tension which characterizes him is released; while in the last analysis only social factors can complete the transformation.' Sartre, J.P. (1965/2008). 'A Plea for the Intellectuals'. In *Between Existentialism and Marxism*. London: Verso, pp. 244–5.

33. Adorno, T.W. (1968/1998). 'Resignation'. In *Critical Models: Interventions and Catchwords*. New York: Columbia University Press, p. 289.

34. Adorno writes, 'people locked in desperately want to get out. In such situations one doesn't think anymore, or does so only under fictive premises. Within absolutized praxis only reaction is possible and therefore false. Only thinking could find an exit, and more a thinking whose results are not stipulated, as is so often the case in discussion in which it is already settled who should be right … if the doors are barricaded, then thought more than ever should not stop short. It is up to thought not to accept the situation as final. The situation can be changed, if at all, by undiminished insight.' Ibid., p. 291.

CHAPTER 8

1. See Said, E. (1996). *Representations of the Intellectual: The 1993 Reith Lectures*. London: Vintage Books; Sartre, 'A Plea for the Intellectuals', pp. 228–85.

2. Freidrich, O. (1981). 'France's Philosopher of Power'. *Time Magazine*. Available at http://web.stanford.edu/class/ihum42/philosopher.pdf

3. Bourdieu, P. (1988). *Homo Academicus*. Stanford: Stanford University Press.

4. Ibid., p. xvii.

5. Bourdieu, P. (1999). *On Television*. New York: New Press, p. 28.

6. A confidential 1985 CIA report on French intellectuals and their connection to the Mitterrand socialist government is interesting in this respect. The report approves of 'nouveaux philosophes' given their hostility to Marxism. In their 'sweeping denunciation of what Levy calls the blindness of the left', the nouveaux philosophes' influence was primarily negative since they had little to offer

in terms of practical suggestions for a new program'. The report celebrates Fernand Braudel and Michel Foucault in the same vein: 'the Annales School turned French historical scholarship on its head in the 1950s and 1960s, primarily by challenging and later rejecting the dominant Marxist theories of historical progress ... In the field of anthropology, the influential structuralist school associated with Claude Levi-Strauss, Foucault among others performed virtually the same mission. We believe their critical demotion of Marxist influence in the social sciences is likely to endure as a profound contribution to modern scholarship ...'. Central Intelligence Agency (1985). 'France: Defection of the Leftist Intellectuals'. Available at www.cia.gov/library/readingroom/docs/CIA-RDP86S00588R000300380001-5. PDF

7. Labaree, D. (2018). 'Gold among the Dross'. *Aeon*. Available at https://aeon.co/amp/essays/higher-education-in-the-us-is-driven-by-a-lust-for-glory?
8. Ibid.
9. Merton, R.K. (1942/1973). 'The Normative Structure of Science'. In Robert K. Merton (ed.), *The Sociology of Science: Theoretical and Empirical Investigations*. Chicago: University of Chicago Press, pp. 255–78.
10. Heesen, R. (2014). 'Three Ways to Become an Academic Superstar'. Working Paper Carnegie Mellon University. Available at https://pdfs.semanticscholar.org/eca8/a27bb81b0f62158ae9f067fb16098f3e022f.pdf
11. Smith, C. (2018). 'How to Be a Prolific Academic: The Writing Strategy of Superstar Scholar, Adam Grant'. *Prolifiko*. Available at https://prolifiko.com/how-to-be-a-prolific-academic-the-writing-strategy-of-superstar-scholar-adam-grant/
12. Newport, C. (2016). *Deep Work: Rules for Focused Success in a Distracted World*. eReader version, accessed 22 December 2019 from Amazon.com.
13. Grant, A. (2017). *Originals: How Non-Conformists Move the World*. eReader version, accessed 22 December 2019 from Amazon.com.
14. Newport, *Deep Work*.
15. Ibid.
16. Ibid.
17. The Chronicle Review (2018). 'How to Fix the Adjunct Crisis'. Available at www.chronicle.com/article/How-to-Fix-the-Adjunct-Crisis/243535

18. Anonymous (2015). 'Academic Superstars: Stop Playing to the Cameras and Get Back to Your Labs'. *Guardian*. Available at www.theguardian.com/higher-education-network/2015/feb/06/academic-superstars-stop-playing-to-the-cameras-and-get-back-to-your-labs

19. See Kimmelman, J. (2009). *Gene Transfer and the Ethics of First-in-Human Experiments: Lost in Translation*. New York: Cambridge University Press.

20. Flam, F. (2019). 'Competitive Culture Is Making Scientists Act Like Awful People'. *Science Alert*. Available at www.sciencealert.com/competitive-culture-is-bringing-out-the-worst-in-scientists-james-watson-crispr-babies/

21. Ibid.

22. Doudna, J. (2019). '100 Most Influential People 2019: He Jiankui'. *Time Magazine*. Available at https://time.com/collection/100-most-influential-people-2019/5567707/he-jiankui/

23. Labaree, 'Gold Among the Dross'.

24. One of the more amusing takes on academic failure was recently articulated by Carl Elliott: 'How to be an academic failure? Let me count the ways. You can become a disgruntled graduate student. You can become a burned-out administrator, perhaps an Associate Dean. You can become an aging, solitary hermit, isolated in your own department, or you can become a media pundit, sought out by reporters but laughed at by your peers. You can exploit your graduate students and make them hate you; you can alienate your colleagues and have them whisper about you behind your back; you can pick fights with university officials and blow your chances at promotion. You can become an idealistic failure at age 25, a cynical failure at 45, or an eccentric failure at 65. If failure is what you're looking for, then you can hardly do better than the academic life. The opportunities are practically limitless.' Elliott, C. (2019). 'How to Be an Academic Failure: An Introduction for Beginners'. *The Ruminator Review*. Available at www.whitecoatblackhat.com/academicfailure/

25. For an excellent and very personal analysis of this silence in US colleges, see bell hook's 'Confronting Class in the Classroom'. In hooks. *Teaching to Transgress*, pp. 177–90.

26. Heesen, R. (2016). 'Academic Superstars: Competent or Lucky?' *Synthese*. 194(11): 4499–518, p. 4499.

27. Featherstone, L. (2019). 'Radical Academics for the Status Quo'. *Jacobin*. Available at https://jacobinmag.com/2019/12/radical-academics-judith-butler-kamala-harris-donation

CHAPTER 9

1. Buchanan and Devletoglou, *Academia in Anarchy*.
2. Ibid., p. 27.
3. In a 1967 press conference, Ronald Reagan criticised certain 'intellectual luxuries' purportedly being enjoyed on rebellious Californian campuses at the taxpayers' expense. When asked to clarify, he replied, 'I would think a course like over at Davis where they teach you to hang the Governor in effigy. That in my mind is an intellectual luxury' (p. 6). Reagan, R. (1967). 'Press Conference of Governor Ronald Reagan Held February 28, 1967'. Available at www.reaganlibrary.gov/digital-library/governor-s-papers-of-the-press-unit
4. Tanzi, A. (2019). 'The Far-Reaching Burden of America's Student Debt'. *Bloomberg*. Available at www.bloomberg.com/news/articles/2019-05-05/-micro-problem-of-student-debt-spurs-suicide-thoughts-survey
5. Student Loan Hero (2019). 'Us Student Loan Debt Statistics for 2019'. Available at https://studentloanhero.com/student-loan-debt-statistics/
6. Ibid.
7. Mitchell, J. (2018). 'Mike Meru Has $1 Million in Student Loans. How Did That Happen?' *Wall Street Journal*. Available at www.wsj.com/articles/mike-meru-has-1-million-in-student-loans-how-did-that-happen-1527252975?mod=e2tw
8. Scott-Clayton, J. (2019). 'The Looming Student Loan Default Crisis Is Worse Than We Thought'. *The Brookings Institute*. Available at www.brookings.edu/research/the-looming-student-loan-default-crisis-is-worse-than-we-thought/
9. McLaughlin, K. (2019). '3 Million Senior Citizens in the US Are Still Paying Off Their Student Loans'. *Business Insider*. Available at www.businessinsider.com.au/americans-over-60-paying-student-loans-2019-5
10. Hoffower, H. (2019). 'Nearly Half of Indebted Millennials Say College Wasn't Worth It, and the Reason Why Is Obvious'. *Business*

Insider. Available at www.businessinsider.com.au/millennials-college-not-worth-student-loan-debt-2019-4

11. Scott-Clayton, 'The Looming Student Loan Default Crisis Is Worse Than We Thought'.

12. Locker, M. (2019). 'Mental Health Survey: 1 in 15 High Student Debt Borrowers Considered Suicide'. *Student Loan Planner*. Available at www.studentloanplanner.com/mental-health-awareness-survey/

13. Ibid.

14. Tanzi, 'The Far-Reaching Burden of America's Student Debt'.

15. Friedman, Z. (2020). 'How COVID-19 Affects Student Loan Forgiveness'. *Forbes*. Available at www.forbes.com/sites/zackfriedman/2020/05/07/student-loan-forgiveness-covid/#2e761c97b043

16. UK Parliament (2019). 'Student Loan Statistics'. Available at https://researchbriefings.parliament.uk/ResearchBriefing/Summary/SN01079

17. BBC (2018). 'Many Graduates Earn "Paltry Returns" for Their Degree'. Available at www.bbc.com/news/education-42923529

18. Ibid.

19. Donelon, M. (2020). 'Universities Minister Calls for True Social Mobility'. Available at www.gov.uk/government/speeches/universities-minister-calls-for-true-social-mobility

20. New Zealand Government (2019). 'Student Loan Scheme Annual Report 2018'. Available at www.educationcounts.govt.nz/publications/80898/student-loan-scheme-annual-report-2018

21. Indeed, it is telling in this regard that China, for example, has no student debt problem, as far as university tuition fees are concerned at least. See Lim, J. (2016). 'Why China Doesn't Have a Student Debt Problem'. *Forbes*. Available at www.forbes.com/sites/jlim/2016/08/29/why-china-doesnt-have-a-student-debt-problem/#20512ec51a58

22. For example, see Schultz, T. (1961). 'Investment in Human Capital.' *The American Economic Review*. 51(1): 1–17.

23. Amazingly, Buchanan even suggests that free tuition represents a wealth transfer from the poor to the rich: 'if measured in terms of wealth – the present value of future earnings – all students become rich relative to those who cannot qualify for admission to universities. In the latter more meaningful sense, the subsidization of university students at the expense of the general taxpayer mounts to a transfer of wealth from the poor to the rich ... event at a broad level

of analysis, free tuition would seem to make the final distribution of income and wealth more, not less, unequal.' Buchanan and Devletoglou, *Academia in Anarchy*, p, 25.

24. Woolley, S. (2019). 'Deutsche Bank Report Says Student Loan Debt Is a "Micro Problem"'. *Bloomberg*. Available at www.bloomberg.com/news/articles/2019-05-01/deutsche-bank-report-says-student-loan-debt-is-a-micro-problem

25. May, T. (2018). 'The Right Education for Everyone'. Available at www.gov.uk/government/speeches/pm-the-right-education-for-everyone

26. It's not surprising that this argument has also been appropriated by conservative government decision-makers, who now see higher education as a class privilege and not a universal right. The UK Prime Minister even questioned whether all young people ought to go to university. Some from poorer backgrounds might pursue more realistic career paths in the trades and service industry. May, 'The Right Education for Everyone'.

27. Save the Student (2019). 'National Student Accommodation Survey 2019'. Available at www.savethestudent.org/accommodation/national-student-accommodation-survey-2019.html

28. Ibid.

29. Packham, A. (2017). 'Students Win £1.5m Pledge from UCL after Five-month Rent Strike'. *Guardian*. Available at www.theguardian.com/education/2017/jul/06/students-win-15m-pledge-from-ucl-after-five-month-rent-strike

30. Fleming, P. (2019). *Sugar Daddy Capitalism: The Dark Side of the New Economy*. Cambridge: Polity.

31. Redfern Legal Centre (2019). 'International Student Workplace Exploitation Widespread'. Available at https://rlc.org.au/article/international-student-workplace-exploitation-widespread

32. ABC News (Four Corners) (2015). 'More Allegations Against 7-Eleven after Malpractice Exposed'. Available at www.youtube.com/watch?v=KBL2Z7G6uq8&t=2s

33. Berg, L. and Farbenblum, B. (2017). 'Wage Theft in Australia: Findings of the National Temporary Migrant Work Survey'. Sydney: Migrant Worker Justice Initiative.

34. Lourenco, D. (2919). 'University of Toronto Students Hold Protest after Third Reported Suicide'. *Vice*. Available at www.vice.com/en_ca/article/j579ax/university-of-toronto-students-hold-protest-after-third-reported-suicide

35. Friesen, J. (2019). 'University of Toronto Installs Safety Barriers after Third Student Suicide in 18 Months'. *The Globe and Mail*. Available at www.theglobeandmail.com/canada/article-university-of-toronto-installs-safety-barriers-after-third-student/

36. Ruben, A. (2018). 'Confessions of a Former Grade Grubber'. *Science Magazine*. Available at www.sciencemag.org/careers/2018/09/confessions-former-grade-grubber

37. For example, see Kellgren, K. (2018). 'Universities Told to End "Spiralling" Grade Inflation'. *BBC*. Available at www.bbc.com/news/education-46604765

38. For an overview of this research, see Schuman, R. (2014). 'Needs Improvement'. *Slate*. Available at https://slate.com/human-interest/2014/04/student-evaluations-of-college-professors-are-biased-and-worthless.html

39. Kornell, N. (2013). 'Do the Best Professors Get the Worst Ratings?' *Psychology Today*. Available at www.psychologytoday.com/au/blog/everybody-is-stupid-except-you/201305/do-the-best-professors-get-the-worst-ratings

40. Bunge, 'Students Evaluating Teachers Doesn't Just Hurt Teachers'.

41. Newton, P. (2018). 'How Common Is Commercial Contract Cheating in Higher Education and Is It Increasing? A Systematic Review'. *Frontiers in Education*. Available at www.frontiersin.org/articles/10.3389/feduc.2018.00067/full

42. BBC (2019). 'How Students Turn to "Essay Mills" to Help Them Cheat'. Available at www.bbc.com/worklife/article/20190329-the-essay-mills-that-help-students-cheat

43. See Gilman, N., Goldhammer, J. and Weber, S. (2011). *Deviant Globalization: Black Market Economy in the 21st Century*. London and New York: Continuum.

CHAPTER 10

1. See Rüegg, Walter (ed.) (2004). *A History of the University in Europe, Volume Three: Universities in the Nineteenth and Early Twentieth Centuries (1800–1945)*. Cambridge: Cambridge University Press.

2. Derrida, J. (2002). 'The University Without Condition'. In *Without Alibi*, Trans Peggy Kamuf. Stanford: Stanford University Press, pp. 202–37; Caplan, *The Case Against Education*.

3. 'To negate a negation does not bring about its reversal'. Adorno, T.W. (1973). *Negative Dialectics*. London: Routledge, p. 159.

4. Adorno and Horkheimer map this sequence from universal reason to specific expressions of social technics (the scientific control and administration of humans) and then onto the horrors of the Marquis de Sade, where cruelty and reason perversely intersect. Life is a gas from there: 'as the transcendental, supraindividual self, reason comprises of the idea of a free, human social life in which men organize themselves as the universal subject and overcome the conflict between pure and empirical reason in the conscious solidarity of the whole ... at the same time. However, reason constitutes the court of judgement of calculation, which adjusts the world for the ends of self-preservation and recognises no other function that the preparation of the object from mere sensory material in order to make it the material of subjugation ... being is apprehended under the aspect of manufacture and administration.' Adorno, T.W. and Horkheimer, M. (1979). *Dialectic of the Enlightenment*. London: Verso, pp. 83–4.

5. US State Department (2019). 'Classes of Nonimmigrants Issued Visas'. Available at https://travel.state.gov/content/dam/visas/ Statistics/AnnualReports/FY2018AnnualReport/FY18Annual Report%20-%20TableXVIA.pdf

6. BBC (2020). 'Coronavirus: Anger over US Decision on Foreign Students' Visas'. Available at www.bbc.com/news/world-us-canada-53320336

7. See Adler and Borys, 'Two Types of Bureaucracy.'

8. See Gouldner, A. (1954). *Patterns of Industrial Bureaucracy: A Case Study of Modern Factory Administration*. New York: Free Press; Blau, P. (1953). *The Dynamics of Bureaucracy: A Study of Interpersonal relations in Two Government Agencies*. Chicago: Chicago University Press.

9. For an excellent analysis of this, see Woodcock, J. (2018). 'Digital Labour in the University: Understanding the Transformations of Academic Work in the UK'. *tripleC*. 16(1). Available at www. triple-c.at/index.php/tripleC/article/view/880

10. Newport, C. (2016). 'A Modest Proposal: Eliminate Email'. *Harvard Business Review*. Available at https://hbr.org/2016/02/a-modest-proposal-eliminate-email

11. Mark, G., Voida, S. and Cardello, A. (2012). 'A Pace Not Dictated by Electrons: An Empirical Study of Work without Email'. *Association for Computing Machinery*. Available at https://sites.oxy.edu/clint/

physio/article/APaceNotDictatedbyElectronsAnEmpiricalStudy ofWorkWithoutEmail.pdf

12. Freire, P. (1970/2009). *Pedagogy of the Oppressed*. New York: Continuum.

13. hooks, *Teaching to Transgress*.

14. Grey, C. (2010). 'Organization Studies: Publications, Politics, Polemic'. *Organization Studies*. 31(6). 677–94, p. 686.

15. For an excellent analysis of how authority and low-cognition can intersect, see Arendt, A. (1971). 'Thinking and Its Moral Considerations'. *Social Research*. 38(3): 417–46.

16. US Department of Education, National Center for Education Statistics (2019). 'The Condition of Education 2019'. NCES 2019-144.

17. American Council on Education (2019). 'Race and Ethnicity in Higher Education Report'. Available at www.equityinhighered.org/resources/report-downloads/

18. Equality and Human Rights Commission (2019). *Tackling Racial Harassment: Universities Challenged*. London: EHRC.

CONCLUSION

1. Tysome, T. (2006). 'Suicide Don under "Huge Stress" on the Job'. *Times Higher Education Supplement*. Available at www.timeshighereducation.com/news/suicide-don-under-huge-stress-in-job/205338.article

2. Andalo, A. (2006). 'Lecturers to Get Counselling Helpline'. *Guardian*. Available at www.theguardian.com/education/2006/sep/20/highereducation.uk

3. See Aronowitz, *The Knowledge Factory*.

4. Marcuse, H. (1955/1967). *Eros and Civilisation: A Philosophical Inquiry into Freud*. New York: Beacon Press, pp. 101–2.

5. Derrida, 'The University Without Condition', pp. 202–37.

6. Ibid., p. 202.

7. Ibid., p. 204.

8. Collini (2012). *What Are Universities For?*

9. Harney and Moten (2013). *The Undercommons*.

10. See Roggero, G. (2011). *The Production of Living Knowledge: The Crisis of the University and the Transformation of Labor in Europe and North America*. Philadelphia: Temple University Press.

11. Harney and Moten, *The Undercommons*, pp. 27–8.

12. See Webb, D. (2018). 'Bolt-Holes and Breathing Spaces in the System: On Forms of Academic Resistance (Or, Can the University Be a Site of Utopian Possibility?)'. *Review of Education, Pedagogy and Cultural Studies*. 40(2): 96–118.
13. A Beckettian political universe, I suggest, is one of enduring the unendurable and putting up with the impossible. This has arguably defined labour's overall response to neoliberalism during the last 35 years. It's best summed up by the famous exchange in *Waiting for Godot*, 'Estragon: I can't go on like this. Vladimir: That's what you think.'
14. See Kant, *Critique of Pure Reason*, p. 677.

Index

n refers to a note

Aaron, Raymond 114
academic capitalism 55, 142, 160, 164
academic celebrities 115–25
academic failures 123, 194*n*24
academic freedom 175*n*41
academics 4–5, 7–8, 19, 23
  and competitive careerism 5, 12, 26
  and conflict of interest with industry 122
  errors by 105
  image of 20–1, 31–2, 45, 156
  impact of metrics on 73–5, 78, 81–2
  and impact partnerships 104–5, 109
  international recruitment of 145
  journal publishing by 49, 78–81
  mental health of 28–9
  personality requirements of 59–60
  research fraud by 80
  status of 177*n*8
  vocation of 27, 37, 116–7, 176*n*5
  workloads of 26–9
adjunct professors 43, 46, 94, 120–1
Adorno, Theodor 110, 144, 192*n*34, 199*n*4
  'Resignation' 110

Althusser, Louis 114
Amazon Corporation 74
American Economic Review 105
Anderson, Malcolm 91–2, 95, 155
arms industry 98
  impact investment by 99–101, 104, 111
  staff and student protests against 103–4
Australia 30–1, 52, 131
  international students in 134–5
Away Days 34–5

BAE Systems 98, 99
Baldwin, James 113
Barcan, Ruth 19, 176*n*5
Beard, Mary 118
Beer, David 70
Bell, Sir David 48
benchmarking 27–8
Bentley University, Mass. 103
Bezos, Jeff 74
Bin Laden, Osama 72
Biswas, Asit and Julian Kirchher
  'Prof, No One is Reading You' 104–5
BlackBerry mobile phones 148
Blau, Peter 147
'boss syndrome' 5, 53, 138
Bourdieu, Pierre *Homo Academicus* 114

Brennan, Jason and Phillip
    Magness *Cracks in the Ivory
    Tower* 44–6
Brexit 144
'broken windows theory' 105
Browne Review (2010) 13
Buchanan, James M. 41, 126–7,
    196*n*23
    Academia in Anarchy 127, 132,
    177–8*n*11
bullying and harassment 60–1,
    91
bureaucratic collectivism 41
    impact on mental health 63–5
Bush, George W. 16
business schools 106
Butler, Judith 125

Campus Living Villages 84, 85
Caplan, Bryan 11, 142
Cato Institute 142
cheating 138–9
Chicago School 90, 127, 131
Childress, Herb 46
Chomsky, Noam 118
Christensen, Clayton 121
collegiality 4, 63, 69, 162–3
Collini, Stefan 162
Columbia University 88
complaints procedures 60–1
contract cheating 138
'cookie monster' experiment
    181*n*15
Coronavirus *see* Covid-19
Covid-19 1
    impact on universities 1–3, 11,
    14, 24, 103, 129, 159–60,
    163
    impact on management 54–5
    impact on volume of email 149

impact on university economy
    38–9, 142
loss of international students
    135, 144–5

dashboards, data collation 66–7,
    72, 73
data-dredging 79–80
Davis, Angela 113
Dawkins Report (Australia 1988)
    19, 131
Day, Ruth 25
De Montfort University 47
Dearing Report (1997) 13, 131
Derrida, Jacques 114, 162, 164
    L'Université sans Condition' 141,
    161–2
Deutsche Bank 132
Devletoglou, Nicos E. 127
DeVos, Betsy 169*n*12
*Diagnostic and Statistical Manual
    of Mental Disorders* 25
Docherty, Thomas 60
Dunleavy, Mile 169*n*15
Duquesne University 93

Edu-Factory 8, 28, 37, 38, 49, 58,
    71, 149, 154
Edwards, Mark 77–8
Eells, Gregory 87–8
Elliott, Carl 194*n*24
Elsevier 46
email 148–50
Emerald Publishing 46
employment, terms and conditions
    of 28, 46, 92–3, 94, 181*n*12
entertainment industry 124
Ernst & Young (EY) 47
Espeland, Wendy 75–6
essay mills 138, 139
EssayShark.com 139

Faculty Land 20
female students, sexual services for rent by 134
Financial Times 150
Fish, Stanley 106–7
Fisher, Mark 63
Fleming, Peter 'Dark academia' 3
Foucault, Michel 113–4
Fox News 142
France, student uprisings in (1968) 110
France Telecom 89
Frankfurt School 110
free tuition 15, 127, 196n23
Freire, Paulo 152
French intellectuals 114–5, 192–3n6

Galloway, Scott 2
Gannon, Kevin 30
Gelsinger, Jesse 122
gender, distribution of professorships by 155–6
Gill, Rosalind 48
Ginsberg, Benjamin *The Fall of the Faculty* 21, 52, 53
Gladwell, Malcolm 115
Glucksmann, André 114
goal displacement 147
Good Will Hunting (film) 156
Goodhart's Law 76
Google Scholar Citation scores 5, 67, 81
Google Talks 115
Gordon, David 56, 57
Gouldner, Alvin 147
grade point averages 45, 136–7
Grant, Adam 119–20
    Originals : How Non-Conformists Move the World 119
Greer, Germaine 115

Grey, Chris 153
Grimm, Stefan 91, 178n12
Guardian, The 150

H-Index 67
Harari, Yuval 120
HARKing 80
Harney, Stefano 32–3, 162, 164
Harris, Kamala 125
Harvey, Stefano 162, 164
Hayek, Friedrich 18, 189n12
    The Road to Serfdom 101
He Jiankui 122
Herndon, Thomas 105
higher education *see* universities
Higher Education Act (US 1992) 131
Hill, Richard 21
Holleran, Madison 88
hooks, bell 30
Horkheimer, Max 144, 199n4
Huffman, Felicity 16, 138
Human Capital Theory 90, 131–2, 134
human resources departments (HR) 61–2, 144
humanities, effect of impact partnerships on 106, 107–8
Humboldtian model, of higher education 17–18, 167n3
Hunter, Thea 94–5

impact investment 99–102, 104, 106, 108–11
Imperial College 26, 91, 178n12
industry, partnerships with universities 35–6, 99–100
information technology 148, 149
intellectuals 113–6, 191–2n32
    see also French intellectuals, public intellectuals

international students 14, 30, 135
  employment of 134–5
  F-1 visas for 144–5
Institute of Art and Ideas 115

Jarratt Report (1985) 18–19, 68
journal article publishing 46,
    78–81, 104
  for career advancement 31, 49
journals
  ranking of 12, 153–4
  ownership by corporations of
    79

K., Anas 17
Kant, Immanuel, on hope 10, 161,
    165
Kay, Andrew 107–8
Kelling, George 105
Keltner, Dacher 56–7
Key Performance Indicators
    (KPIs) 35, 55
Klein, Naomi 121
Knight, Frank 127
knowledge, capitalising of 35
Kong, Olivia 25

Labaree, David 116, 117, 122–3
LaBerge, Leigh Claire 47
league tables 150
lecturers 26–7, 151–2
  conditions of employment 3,
    28, 43, 46
  evaluation by students of 77,
    137–8
  ranking of 71–2, 73
Lee, Oliver 29
Lévy, Bernard-Henri 114
Lewis, Nick 20
Likert Scale 77
Lockheed Martin 98, 99, 103

London Review of Books 124
Lorde (singer) 67
Lorenz, Chris 69
Loughlin, Lori 16, 138
Lukianoff, Greg and Heidt,
    Jonathan The Coddling of the
    American Mind 32
Lyon 2 University 16

McGlyn, Terry 120–1
McKinsey & Co. 47
management accounting, digitisa-
    tion of 68
Marcuse, Herbert 161
Marinetto, Mike 31
market individualisation 41, 43,
    86
May, Theresa 132
measurement, manipulation of
    77–8
Meehan, Marty 99
merit awards 69–70
Merton, Robert 117
metrics 66–9, 72–3, 81, 153
Mexico Wall 144
Morrish, Liz 27
Moten, Fred 32–3, 118, 162, 164
Motlagh, Kristine 129
Muller, Jerry 67, 72
Myriad Genetics Inc. 109

National Health Service (NHS)
    102
National Union of Students,
    report on student accommo-
    dation 133
Nature (journal) 26
neoclassical economics 41, 56,
    101, 114
  and employment relationships
    69

neoliberalism 4, 11, 18–19, 22
    impact on employment
      relations 62
    impact on mental health 63–4,
      90–1
New Public Management (NPM)
    40–3, 146, 161
New York Times 74, 124
New Zealand, student debt in 131
Newport, Cal *Deep Work* 119
Nixon, Richard 127
non-disclosure agreements 62–3

Obama, Barack, 'College
    Scorecard' system 68
Office 365 23
Oxford University Press (OUP)
    46

P-hacking 79–80
Pendrous, Mason 83–4, 86
pensions schemes, strikes over cuts
    to 6–7, 8–9, 62, 161
Performance Improvement Plans
    67
performance indicators 35, 55–6,
    72
performance metrics 72–3, 75–6,
    81
perverse incentives 76, 77–8
Peterson, Jordan 156
    12 Rules for Life 113
philosophy 106–7
plagiarism 138–9
post-graduate students 26, 35–6
power, impact on behaviour of
    57, 60
Principal Investigator (PI) 121
Pritchett, Wendell 87–8
private colleges 43, 102, 145–6
    accreditation of 169*n*12

Public Choice Theory 41, 45, 126,
    177–8*n*11
public intellectuals 113–5, 191*n*32
publishing houses 46, 179*n*20

QS World University Rankings
    68
quantification 70–1, 77, 81, 143
Queen Mary University 28

race, distribution of professorships
    by 155–6
'rank and yank' 74
ranking systems 74–5, 150–1
Ranking Web of Universities 150
Raytheon Company 98, 103–4
Raytheon UMass Lowell
      Research Institute (RURI)
      99, 101, 103
Readings, Bill T*he University in
      Ruins* 21, 178–9*n*17
Reagan, Ronald 127, 128, 195*n*3
Reinhart, Carmen 105
Research Excellence Framework
    68, 70, 99
Rhodes, Carl 175*n*41
Robbins, Lionel, Baron Robbins
    18
Robbins Report (1963) 18
Rogoff, Kenneth 105
Rovelli, Carlo 120
Roy, Siddharta 77–8
Russell, Bertrand 113
Russell Group 151

SafeAssign (plagiarism detection
      system) 138
Sage Publishing 46
Sandberg, Sheryl 119
Sanders, Bernie 125
Sartre, Jean-Paul 113, 191–2*n*32

Sauder, Michael 75–6
Saudi Arabia, bombing of Yemen by 97–8
scholars *see* academics
Schröder-Turk, Gerd 30
Science (journal) 80
Seekingarrangement.com 134
Shapiro, Ben 11
Shore, Cris 20, 42
Singer, William Rick 16
Snow, C.P. *The Masters* 156
Sontag, Susan 113
Southern University of Science and Technology 122
Soviet Union 71
Srigley, Ron 59–60
stack-ranking 74, 75, 150
Stakhanovite movement 71
Stanford University 16
Stapel, Diederik 80–1
STEM subjects (Science, Technology, Engineering, Mathematics) 36, 106
student accommodation 85, 133–4
student loans and debt 13–14, 16, 128–33
links to mental health disorders 128–9
students
behaviour in class of 29
class attendance by 86–7
employment of 134–5
evaluation of lecturers by 77, 138
mental health of 24–6, 89, 133
protest movements (1960s) 126–7
welfare of 84–6
see also international students, post-graduate students, undergraduate students

suicide 48, 89
by academics 87–8, 91, 159
by students 25, 31, 48, 88–9, 136
supervisors 56, 59

Taylorism 54
teachers *see* lecturers
TED Talks 115
Thatcher, Margaret 128
'Three Ways to Become an Academic Superstar' 118
Time (magazine) 114, 115, 122
Times Higher Education World University Rankings 68
Todd Report (NZ 1994) 19, 131
trade unions 160–1
Trump, Donald Jr. 156
tuition fees 14, 19, 127, 132, 151
Turnitin (plagiarism detection system) 138

undercommons 163, 164
undergraduate students 24, 25
United States 14, 16, 93, 94
Ivy League colleges 16
private colleges in 14
universities
administration personnel 51–3, 147–8
authoritarianism in 4, 33–7, 53, 56, 121
bribery for admission to 16
bureaucratisation of 14, 21, 53, 56, 59, 147
businessification of 36, 43, 145, 178–9n17
class sizes in 151, 152
commercialisation of 15, 17, 22–3, 38–40, 48, 101, 146
commodification of 137, 139, 161

corporatisation of 5, 12, 15, 38,
47–8, 51, 142, 146–7
government policies on 13, 15
and impact partnerships 35,
99–102, 104, 108–10
investment ventures by 47–8
managerialism in 23, 28–9, 54
marketisation of 39–40, 146
non-academic personnel 14,
51–2
in post-WWII period 15, 18,
160, 161–2
purpose of 160, 161–2
rankings of 68, 76, 150–1
salaries of senior executives 47,
52
unofficial formal/informal
culture in 143
see also academics, higher
education, lecturers
University of Adelaide 103
partnership with Lockheed
Martin 103
University of Alaska 13, 169n15
University of Bristol
suicide of students at 25, 88, 89
University of California, Berkeley
71
University of Canterbury (NZ) 83
University of Cardiff 91, 155
University College London 133–4
University of Coventry 7
University of Liverpool 9
University of Massachusetts
Lowell 111
partnership with Raytheon 98–9

University of Pennsylvania 25,
88
gene therapy experiments at
122
University of Reading 48
University of Toronto 136
University of Utah 109
University of Warwick 60
'university without conditions'
161–2, 164
US News and World Report Best
Colleges 68

Vietnam War, student protests
against 126
Vojtko, Margaret Mary 93–4

Walsh, Jack 77
Warner, Marina 51
Washburn, Jennifer 109
Washington Consensus 139, 144
Weber, Max 'The Scholar's Work'
167n3
West, David 60–1
Western Connecticut State
University 94
Whatsyourprice.com 134
Wilson, James 105
work, types of 57–9
work/life balance 154–5

Yale University 16
Yemen, bombing by Saudi Arabia
of 97–8

Žižek, Slavoj 113